Confessions of a Teenage Witch

Confessions of a Teenage Witch

CELEBRATING THE WICCAN LIFE

Gwinevere Rain

A Perigee Book

THE BERKLEY PUBLISHING GROUP
Published by the Penguin Group
Penguin Group (USA) Inc.
375 Hudson Street, New York, New York 10014, USA
Penguin Group (Canada), 10 Alcorn Avenue, Toronto, Ontario M4V 3B2, Canada
(a division of Pearson Penguin Canada Inc.)
Penguin Books Ltd., 80 Strand, London WC2R 0RL, England
Penguin Group (Ireland), 25 St. Stephen's Green, Dublin 2, Ireland (a division of Penguin Books Ltd.)
Penguin Group (Australia), 250 Camberwell Road, Camberwell, Victoria 3124, Australia
(a division of Pearson Australia Group Pty. Ltd.)
Penguin Books India Pvt. Ltd., 11 Community Centre, Panchsheel Park, New Delhi—110 017, India
Penguin Books (NZ), cnr. Airborne and Rosedale Roads, Albany, Auckland 1310, New Zealand
(a division of Pearson New Zealand Ltd.)
Penguin Books (South Africa) (Pty.) Ltd., 24 Sturdee Avenue, Rosebank, Johannesburg 2196,
South Africa
Penguin Books Ltd., Registered Offices: 80 Strand, London WC2R 0RL, England

Copyright © 2005 by Catherine Williams
Cover art and design by Ben Gibson

PRINTING HISTORY
Perigee trade paperback edition / July 2005

ISBN: 0-399-53161-0

PERIGEE is a registered trademark of Penguin Group (USA) Inc.
The "P" design is a trademark belonging to Penguin Group (USA) Inc.

This book has been catalogued by the Library of Congress

PRINTED IN THE UNITED STATES OF AMERICA

10   9   8   7   6   5   4   3   2   1

Book Blessing

Upon a midnight hour
I weave a web of power
cast the night of October's Blood Moon
to evoke a magical boon
I ask that the Great Divine
bless each passage and every line
and help those who seek a new way
find the serenity of a starlite bay
present, future, past
I make this spell to last
so mote it be!

Contents

 Part One

Part Two

Acknowledgments

Much love and thanks to my family and friends who have generously supported my writing. To my mother, Ann, for her continued guidance; author Scott Cunningham whose words first illuminated my path; M.R. for always listening; and Christel Winkler, editor extraordinaire.

I'd especially like to acknowledge the following teens for lending their voice to this guide: Gede, Deborah, Janni, Katelyn, Eric, Gianluca, and Abel. May your contributions bring warmth to others on their magical journey.

Finally to my Goddess and God for sending your divine rays of inspiration and perseverance. Blessings to you all!

Preface

I have a confession to make: Being Wiccan is much more challenging than I initially thought. Yet one of the things that makes this path so fulfilling is overcoming these challenges. In the six years that I have been practicing, I've had profound lessons and perfect moments of clarity. I truly believe that I am meant to share these revelations and experiences with you. However, only conveying positive outcomes would be like telling half of a story. This is why I promise to be real, honest, fearless, go deep down inside myself, and confess *everything*.

Such personal insight may sound enticing, but to truly embrace your *own* journey I've enclosed practical, useful material and enriched guidance so you may learn the diverse aspects of Wicca, spark an ongoing internal discussion, and tap into the magical power of intuition.

We will explore this beautiful religion—its meaning, concepts, and ideas. *Confessions of a Teenage Witch* invites you to take the integral step from novice to practitioner. It is time for you to reach beyond the basics and understand what lessons and skills you'll need to not only practice the path, but to live the path.

This book is divided into two parts. The first is informative, containing advice and musings in regard to Wiccan practice and teen life. The second half is similar to a workbook, with step-by-step ritual instructions and magick spells.

Additionally, the sidebars of this text contain direct quotes from my Book of Shadows, and contain witchy confessions, memories, mishaps, and triumphs. Input and stories from other teen Wiccans will round out this versatile primer. *Confessions of a Teenage Witch* can be read either in order or by randomly selecting chapters at your own discretion.

Introduction

Upon starting my Wiccan journey at the age of fourteen, I knew I would have a lot to learn. I was asking myself serious questions: What do I believe in? How should I envision Divinity? Will being a Wiccan alter my personality or affect the way I live my life? Those kinds of questions arose daily but I focused on the specific purpose for this change: to be happy and fulfilled. I considered my future as a Wiccan, pondering what twists and turns would come my way. When I approached a difficult point in my studies, I persisted. My mantra became, *Don't give up, don't be discouraged*. It was all so new and different. Change may shake a person up but it also frees them.

Being a Wiccan practitioner, walking the path, and sometimes stumbling is a spiritual discovery of the mind, body, and soul. I found a religion that fit perfectly but through that search I also found missing parts of myself. Wicca didn't change me; in fact, it helped me realize the core of who I am, so I could embrace my true self, aspire to be a more gentler, kinder person, and seek my deepest desires. Ultimately, I came to understand that Wicca is as much about having a belief in yourself as it is in the higher powers.

Some adult practitioners may brush us off because we are young, but we are lucky because our age compels us to have an open mind. Being teenagers is about exploring who we are and what the world holds. Youth lends us passion and vigor. What you do with that energy lies within your hands, but as Wiccans we know that magick is a perfect way to harness, control, and evoke that power source.

Working with spells (magick) is a skill slowly built and cultivated through practice, experimentation, and persistence. Being Wiccan also requires the use of these things. We adapt and grow as our path changes or shifts into a new direction. In the beginning, each day comes with new lessons but eventually most practitioners find themselves wanting more. They feel a need to move beyond basic Wicca and expand their path.

Would you like to shed the beginner image? Evolve into an intermediate practitioner? Become a priest or priestess of this path? If you truly believe this religion is meant to be a part of your life then I would like to help you achieve this goal. I know you have the ability; it is within you, aching to be released.

The path of the intermediate isn't always easy but it gives many Wiccans deep meaning and fulfillment. Priest- or priestesshood is a process of coming into yourself as a person, releasing doubt, and gaining focus. I believe each person has an individual experience, which makes these terms difficult to define. In my opinion, being an intermediate practitioner is about listening to your soul, living the path, believing in ethics, honoring the Goddess and God, following the wheel of the year, and rhythm of the moon.

From this point forward I want you to put the terms *beginner*, *newbie*, and *novice* behind you because with help from this book you will no longer need those words to define yourself. It is time to take action, combine the lessons you will learn, and successfully apply them to your life and practice. Now you are on your way to becoming a priest or priestess of Wicca. Welcome to the next step on your magical journey!

Meet the Contributors

Gede Parma is fifteen, male and lives in Queensland, Australia. He first heard the word *Wicca* at school when a peer in his class expressed it was his religion. Gede said, "What primarily attracted me to the religion was that it involved working with magick and my own inner power. It helped me get through some pretty hard times during my first years of high school."

Deborah Painter, a.k.a. Ariawn, is nineteen, female and lives in Ohio. Her best friend discussed Wicca with Deborah over breakfast one morning at McDonald's. She recounts the experience saying, "What she told me awakened the spark of spirit I had been missing for so long."

Janni Ingman, a.k.a. Luna, is sixteen, female and lives in Finland. She came across Wicca via the Internet and conveyed,

"We can each find our own way and learn to use the magick within."

Katelyn Dreux, a.k.a. Lynx Song, is fifteen, female and lives in Louisiana. She learned about Wicca during a visit to her local bookstore where she came upon a popular Wiccan book for teens. It took her a year before she went back and purchased it. Katelyn said, "I love that the religion doesn't preach one true way or hold an emphasis on masculine over feminine."

Eric Wheeler, a.k.a. Chiron Nightwolf, is sixteen, male and lives in Georgia. He was drawn to Wicca because the ideology matched his personal beliefs. Eric runs an Internet support group for young adult practitioners on MSN called Teen Wicca Sanctuary. When asked who he turns to for guidance, he replied, "My friends online, to get advice from people who are going through the same thing."

Gianluca Lou, a.k.a. Pytho, is fourteen, male and lives in Milan, Italy. He found Wicca through "an investigation of the lesser-known spiritual practices of the world." He believes that, "true spirituality and understanding of religion comes from the inside."

Abel Rene Gomez, a.k.a. Anubis RainHawk, is fifteen, male and lives in California. When the first Harry Potter book was published, his peers at school were enchanted by mythical wizardry, but Abel decided to research the real religion of Wicca. He recalled, "I surfed websites, visited libraries, and discussed it with friends and family. . . . I was taken on a mystical journey of enlightenment and fulfillment. I was immersed into a world of magick, mystery, and endless exploration."

ONE

Wiccan Essentials

I want to take a few moments to express the terminology and vocabulary used throughout this book. Please note that these are my personal views and definitions.

Pagan: Practitioner of an earth-centered religion. Modern-day pagans often look beyond traditional Christian, Islamic, and Judaic teachings, and focus on Eastern philosophies and healing techniques.

Wicca: A nature-influenced (Pagan) religion with practitioners believing in duel deities—a Goddess and God. Its basic tenants include the Rede "An ye harm none," and Rule of Three, "What energies you send out eventually return three-fold." *Wiccan* refers to a person (male or female) who honors and follows the religion along with its rules. Sometimes I'll use the term *practitioner* interchangeably with Wiccan.

Witch: Used to illustrate a person (male or female) who utilizes *Witchcraft*, the art and craft of magick. There are several types of Witches: Hereditary Witch, Green Witch, Eclectic Witch, etc.

Within this book I have chosen to focus on **Solitary Wiccan Witches.** These people are practitioners of Wicca who primarily practice alone and abide by the Rede. My emphasis on Solitary Wiccan Witches is not to exclude other types of Witches. Instead, it is used to promote positive magick and ethical guidelines. Since I am a Solitary Wiccan Witch, it will set the focus and theme of this guide.

Craft: A term used to identify any Pagan-based path or practice. Also used as an abbreviated form of Witchcraft or the Wiccan Craft.

Quick Wicca Q&A

What follows is an extensive batch of beginner's questions. Many of the responses cover Wiccan basics and are a source of review for more experienced practitioners. I compiled the questions by reviewing my personal correspondences, both e-mails and letters, which were sent by teens starting on the Wiccan path.

Where did Wicca originate? How did it begin? What other paths does Wicca relate to?

Wicca was first started in England by a man named Gerald Gardner in the 1950s. Many people link Wicca to the druids, ceremonialism, and shamanism, as well as ancient Celtic practices. Even though Wiccan rituals and methods might have a common thread with these groups, it does not necessarily mean that they are connected. It is believed that Gardner added teachings and philosophies from other paths when forming the religion.

How does someone become Wiccan?

In order to become Wiccan a person consciously decides for him or herself that the path is correct for them. Calling oneself Wiccan means that you are identifying Wicca as your religion, and honor its guidelines.

Are there any age requirements for being Wiccan?

People find Wicca at different stages in life. Men and women in their late fifties may just be realizing its presence for the first time. Likewise, young people around twelve are also finding Wicca. There is no age requirement. However, parents sometimes object to their children's interest and covens are often reluctant to let teens join. These issues can make it difficult for younger people to practice, but not impossible.

Do you need to be initiated?

Years ago it was believed that the only way to join Wicca was to be initiated by another practitioner. Within the past two decades this thought pattern has changed dramatically. Some solitary practitioners use self-initiation rituals and others like myself see no need to have any sort of initiation. You are a Wiccan through practice, honoring the Wiccan Rede and having true knowledge of the Craft.

How do Wiccans view God/deity?

Unlike other religions that only believe in a supreme male God, Wiccans see deity in two parts—Goddess (feminine) and God (masculine). We honor these energies equally and believe they exist everywhere, especially in nature and inside each human being. Prayer, meditation, and rituals are used to connect with the higher powers. (See chapter Two for more details on how Wiccans view deity.)

What are some myths and stereotypes that challenge Wiccans?

There are several main stereotypes associated with Wicca: that we perform blood sacrifices, fly on broomsticks, or want to curse everyone. Wiccans don't partake in any of these events. Instead we seek to grow as individuals, using prayer, meditation, creative visualization, and positive spells to improve our lives. Each day Wiccans continually try to combat negative projections and seek to show the path in its true light.

What sets Wicca apart from other religions?

Wicca doesn't have a central holy book or scripture. Instead we use common sense and the ethical guideline, harm none and adhere to the basic idea of Karma: the energies you send out, you will eventually receive back. In addition, Wicca is very empowering, especially to women who feel they have been oppressed by other religious paths. Basically, the unique values, ideas, and concepts continue to draw practitioners, and make Wicca one of the fastest growing religions in the United States.

Do Wiccans worship the Devil or Satan?

Wiccans do not worship an evil entity such as the Christian Devil or Satan. We realize that there are negative influences and bad people in this world, but instead of blaming behavior or problems on a mythical demon we believe in taking personal responsibility.

Does being Wiccan cost money?

Apart from the occasional book or tool, being Wiccan does not cost money. There are thrifty ways to find (or make) altar tools. Used books can be located online at auction sites, and new age stores sometimes provide free Wicca 101 lessons (although it's always a good idea to ask beforehand if there will be a fee). Covens occasionally ask for donations, and festivals charge attendees to help cover expenses.

What holidays do Wiccans celebrate?

Wiccans celebrate eight special days each year. These Sabbats—Yule, Imbolc, Ostara, Beltane, Litha, Lughnasadh, Mabon, and Samhain—reflect seasonal changes and symbolically represent the birth, life, death and rebirth of the God figure. (For in-depth holiday information and observance dates, see chapter Seven.)

How did the Sabbats originate?

Many believe that the Wiccan holidays grew out of northern European and ancient Celtic traditions. However, it is hard to definitively say. What we do know is that in order to honor the Earth's changes, our Sabbats mark important seasonal transitions. No matter where they originated from, the holidays hold special meaning for Wiccans. They are sacred days, which are used to pay tribute to the higher powers.

Can Wiccans still celebrate Christmas or Hanukkah with family members or will that upset the higher powers?

Many Wiccans have family members who are Christian, Catholic, or Jewish so they are familiar with family customs such as Christmas and Hanukkah. Often Wiccans take time to reflect on the importance of family instead of that day's particular religious connotation. Celebrating Christmas or Hanukkah with family is also a good way to show tolerance and respect. Hopefully those same nonWiccan family members will return the favor and become more tolerant of the Wiccan ways. Don't worry about upsetting the Goddess and God, I believe they understand the importance of togetherness.

Why is Magick spelt with a k?

Many Wiccans see a need to separate stage magic and spellcraft. This alternative spelling supposedly originates from ceremonialist Aleister Crowley. Adding on the "k" immediately tells people that the subject is about spells, not about a rabbit being pulled out of a hat. Although not as common, others may use the spellings Majick or Majik. Whichever method you decide upon, remember that they all mean the same thing!

What are correspondences?

Correspondence is a term used in Wicca that means magical association. It is a way to link energies, concepts, and intent. For example, green is a color often connected with money; therefore, green is a correspondence of financial goals and prosperity spells. Correspondences can be attributed to herbs, oils, planetary influences, moon phases, days of the week, and more!

What are the elements? And what do they have to do with Magick?

The elements are: Earth, Air, Fire, and Water. Since we need each of these essential elements to survive, their energies are said to hold power. During magick practice and circle casting we draw upon elemental energies to aid us in our task. Ultimately, using the elements helps practitioners align themselves with the universe.

Are male Witches or Wiccans called Warlocks?

In either Craft guys are not called Warlocks. This is a common myth that doesn't seem to go away! In fact, in ancient times the term was used negatively. Male practitioners are always called Wiccans or Witches. Except in the case of "priest" and "priest-ess," there aren't any further title distinctions between males and females.

What does the pentacle represent and is it evil?

The pentacle is a five-pointed star encased within a circle. Each point of the star represents one of the four elements (Earth, Air, Fire, and Water), and the fifth point signifies Akasha (meaning, spirit). The circle is representative of cycles: the moon cycle, seasonal cycle, as well as the cycles of life, death, and rebirth. Pentacles are symbols mainly used for protection and purification. Often worn as jewelry (for both men and women) or placed on the altar to bless and consecrate objects, this Wiccan symbol is not evil; in fact, it brings practitioners a sense of comfort, empowerment, and confidence.

What is visualization?

Visualization is a process of strongly picturing an image in your mind. Usually practitioners visualize during spells, rituals, or meditation exercise. The purpose of visualization is to focus on a specific goal and direct intent in order to aid a desired outcome. Visualization is a skill slowly built up and enhanced over time. If a white mist becomes a challenge to mentally conjure, then aim for white snowflakes or sparks. Once you can picture or "see" the goal in your mind, then your desire will know how to manifest.

Is there a book that could be described as a Bible for Wiccans?

The term *bible* is often connected to Catholicism/Christianity. Since Wicca isn't a part of these paths it is difficult to assign this label to specific texts or scriptures in conjunction with Wicca. Although many books have been published on the topic of Wicca and practitioners refer to them for information, there is no central authoritative holy book in this path. Aside from those published sources, many Wiccans keep what is called a Book of Shadows.

What is a Book of Shadows?

A Book of Shadows is a journal that is created and used by practitioners of Wicca. Each person has the option of using one and many choose to take advantage of its benefits. Inside a Book of Shadows, one might find a record of spells, prayers, invocations, and magical experiences. However, personal reflections, holidays, rituals, deity info, and dream notes are often the main focus. Since a Wiccan's Book of Shadows is considered to be sacred, many keep it stashed away in a safe place. (See end of this chapter for a special section on how to create your own Book of Shadows.)

Gwinevere, why were you initially drawn to Wicca?

Several attributes caught my eye; I noticed that this religion allows practitioners to mold the path to fit their individual needs. I love the concept of honoring a Goddess. As a young woman, I craved to know a higher feminine power. Wicca provided that comfort. Magick as a source of empowerment also helped fuel my desire to become Wiccan. Each of these concepts drew me to the path and continue to hold my interest.

What is a coven?

A coven consists of three or more practitioners who gather together and cast magick, celebrate holidays, and perform Full Moon rituals. Generally they are lead by a High Priestess and/or a High Priest. Coven meetings average about once or twice a month.

What are the basics of meditation?

Meditation is a healthy practice that can help enhance one's concentration and psychic awareness. There are several key preparations before starting a meditation session. First, the atmosphere that is best is a peaceful and private one. Consider using subtle lighting and gentle music (preferably music without lyrics, such as sounds of nature or trancelike rhythms) to further create the mood. During my meditations, I prefer to use about two to three candles and keep them in a safe, sturdy place. I want all of my focus to be on the exercise instead of worrying whether they might tip over.

Some Wiccans emphasize a specific position for meditation. I believe that a person's comfort level is most important. Try several different poses—sitting cross-legged, lying stretched out on the bed, kneeling on a cushion—to find out which one works best. The goal of meditation is to become calm and centered. For guided excercies, you may want to record yourself reading the passage then play the tape back to partake in the exercise, or read it over a few times to get a feel for the imagery and direction. You don't have to memorize every detail but it is important to slowly progress into the meditation and come out of it in a similar fashion.

Are Wiccans supposed to convert nonpractitioners to the path?

No, Wiccans don't proselytize. Since free will is an essential aspect of this path, we believe that each person should find the religion that appeals to them without being pushed into a specific path. In the end, the faith they choose may or may not be Wicca.

What is dogma and how does it relate to Wicca?

This term occasionally pops up in various Wiccan books. Dogma is a set of beliefs or creeds. The Wiccan Rede and Rule of Three would be considered Wiccan dogma. Dogmatic and dogmatism have more negative connotations. These phrases roughly mean that a person or group of people have strongly held, rigid beliefs. Often these people express them in a harsh manner that suggests their philosophy should be accepted without question or considering another's interpretation.

What advice do you give to those who are looking to become Wiccan?

My best advice is to follow your heart and listen to your intuition. Only you know what's best for yourself, and what you want to achieve in life. Read about Wicca in depth, as this path should be seriously understood before you make any big choices. If you do feel Wicca is the religion meant for you, remember to honor the Wiccan Rede along with your own personal ethics.

Finding Your Craft Name

For many practitioners, a Craft name marks the transition and entrance onto the Wiccan path. In essence it is used to represent the birth of a new magical you! Additionally, some feel that the name bestowed on them at birth doesn't fit their personality. To supplement what a given name may lack, one might pick a Craft name with deep symbolism and meaning to truly reflect their inner spirt. Having a Craft name isn't meant to deny or replace your birth name. If you feel a Craft name doesn't serve a purpose in your life that's okay, too, because this practice is completely optional.

There are several ways to select a Craft name. Please realize that this process varies by person and may take several attempts. Consider the following techniques:

Dream Work. One night, keep a notebook (or your Book of Shadows) and pen beside your bed. Before you go to sleep, ask the Goddess and God to send you your magical name. Upon waking, record any dream you may have had, paying close attention to embedded symbols and messages.

Divination. Continuously working with tarot, runes, etc., can be helpful in choosing a Craft name because it opens your psychic mind, drawing out hidden imagery.

Word Association. On a separate sheet of paper write down your initial impression of the following words. Don't overanalyze these concepts, just write the first thing that pops into your mind: *Goddess; Wicca; Magick; God; Mystery; Creative; Beauty; Spells; Eternal; Craft.*

Reflect on the key words you wrote during this exercise. Why did you chose them? What do they say about your quest for a magical name and journey into Wicca?

Chanting. Repeating a phrase or spoken charm will push aside your analytical mind and awaken your subconscious. Remember to quickly write down symbols or words that stood out during your rhythmic chanting.

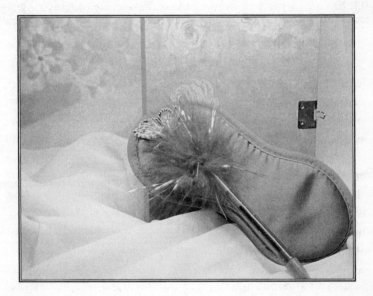

🌿 From Gwinevere's Book of Shadows

July 9, 2000—Age 15

It's been about a year that I've practiced Wicca. I've learned so much about myself and this beautiful path. Throughout this time I've taken different craft names: "Rain," then "Coyote Rain," but now I've become Gwinevere Rain

> 🌿 **From Gwinevere's Book of Shadows**
>
> *May 3, 2004—Age 19*
>
> I was reviewing my old Book of Shadows entries and came across several passages signed "Coyote Rain." What was I thinking? I am so thankful I kept pursuing my magical name because Gwinevere Rain has molded into a part of my identity, as a person, a Wiccan, and a writer.

Guided Meditation/Pathworking. Search for written stories with predetermined visualizations, on the Internet or in Wicca books. These meditations take you into a world of fantasy and imagination, a perfect place to find your new Craft name.

Favorite Things. Perhaps the easiest method entails jotting down a list of your favorite things. Think of colors, the elements, animals, celestial bodies, gemstones, crystals, nature, flowers, and herbs, then combine two or three of those concepts together. See which words form creative links. For example names like "Sagewolf" or "Citrine Rose" are original and expressive.

Other methods include delving into mythology, casting a spell, or consulting numerology. Whether you combine several unique words or decide upon a single term, your Craft name has the potential to shine the light from your soul into the outer world. If you're having difficulties, don't despair. With time and determination, you'll find your Craft name. It might even find you!

Finding my craft name was an extremely difficult process. I decided to ask Deity for help. I asked my spirit guide and guardian angels for guidance as well.
—Anubis RainHawk, age 15, California, USA

Whenever I read in different books about finding a Craft name I always felt anxious that I hadn't found mine yet. So, I tried to force a name to come to me. It never worked; all the names I tried just didn't seem to fit. Some things you can't force. All you can do is wait.
—Lynx Song, age 15, Louisiana, USA

Creating a Book of Shadows

Perhaps the most personal tool used in Wicca is the practitioner's Book of Shadows which tracks his or her journey, yet it is more than a source for keeping records. The Book of Shadows (also referred to by its initials BOS) is an intimate written portrayal, filled with one-of-a-kind magical experiences.

If you're concerned about starting a Book of Shadows for fear that it won't be "good enough," push those doubts and hesitation aside. What makes the book sacred and special isn't its perfect appearance or organization; instead, it's the practitioner's love and effort that enchants its pages. What follows are my suggestions on a book's creation; feel free to customize them to suit your individual needs.

Crafting the Book

You have several material options for making your Book of Shadows. Of course, your choice will vary upon intention and

---

❧ From Gwinevere's Book of Shadows

October 9, 2000—Age 16

I could stay up all night and write in my Book of Shadows. I recently purchased it to make a fresh start. The pen glides across the paper and my thoughts are clear and true. I already feel like my opinions are validated.

---

access to supplies but also remember to consider your level of comfort since you'll be writing in it often. If you're left-handed a hardbound book may prove to be a challenge as you'll probably struggle against the inside spine. When reviewing the items below, assess their pros and cons to make the best decision.

Diary with Lock and Key. If you use this type of book you'll be able to keep magical thoughts safely stashed away. If privacy is especially an issue (perhaps you share a room with a sibling) then this option might be your best choice.

Spiral-Bound Journal. If you're seeking a Book of Shadows that lays flat and allows you to easily tear out paper without loosening the binding, then a spiral book may suit your needs. Remember to organize the sections carefully, allowing enough pages per topic.

Three-Ring Binder. My Book of Shadows is in this format. It is highly functional (you can remove and add papers at your will) and allows you to express your creativity through various decorating options (see the next page for more details). The only negative is its big and bulky size, which can be difficult to work with in a squished circle or altar space.

Hardbound Book. Although beautiful to look at, the hardbound book proves to be a difficult item to work with. Tear out a couple pages and the inner binding may start to fall apart or the book won't stay open when you're trying to perform a ritual. If your heart is set on a beautiful hardbound book, utilize one to keep your daily magical thoughts and a binder for rituals and growing information.

Floppy Disk/CD-ROM. If you are technologically savvy and prefer typing over writing by hand then using a floppy disk or CD-ROM to hold your info may be your best Book of Shadows option. However, this efficient method can also have its downside because you won't have a paper copy to consult during rituals, so consider typing, editing, and then printing your journal entries and witchy information. This way you'll have an easy-to-read hard copy and saved document.

My first Book of Shadows was a binder, compiled with several sections. I find binders easier to organize and search for certain information. However, there was a point where I felt my binder could no longer sustain my needs. I now have a hardback book, which I use to write down the most significant of rituals and experiences.

—PYTHO, AGE 14, MILAN, ITALY

ORGANIZE AND DECORATE

Creating different sections in your Book of Shadows helps maintain a level of organization. If you're using a binder as your Book of Shadows, divider sheets with tabs are really helpful. At a moment's glance you'll be able to find the right material. For bound books, either glue on handmade tabs or fold a page in half to mark the beginning of a new section. Below, you'll find more tips on creating BOS sections.

Purchasing or decorating paper for your book's interior can make a personalized statement. If you're using a binder, the right paper selection can also help avoid an undesired school feeling.

Office supply stores have whole aisles dedicated to fancy paper of varying shades, and many craft stores carry really cool scrapbooking supplies. Visit different places for a shopping adventure. To make your Book of Shadows shine like a rainbow, use different colors for each section!

Decorating blank printer or looseleaf paper by hand can be an inexpensive alternative. Add stickers, paste pictures from magazines, and release the artist within by using stamps, crayons, or colored pencils.

Once you've purchased or decorated paper you'll probably need a hole puncher to insert them into your binder. Look for a three-hole punch at your local office supply store. They are likely to carry this item for fewer than ten dollars, and since it's a onetime purchase with benefits including ease

> ### ❧ From Gwinevere's Book of Shadows
> *August 16, 1999—Age 15*
> After searching my Book of Shadows for a good twenty minutes, I realized how desperately I needed some BOS organization. This is why I created a ritual and spell sheet, to detail whenever I cast a spell or ritual and the reason why. I will be able to keep track of my witchy happenings without having to fumble through my book, wondering if I performed a Sabbat ritual the previous month. Additionally, this will prove to be a great help in establishing how many spells I perform and the exact day when they were cast.

of use, organization, and the ability to add pages at your own pace, you won't regret the decision.

BOOK SECTIONS

The sections in your Book of Shadows are comparable to chapters in a novel. They help break up text and make an organized, efficient read. To get the most out of your sections, you'll want to make them transition smoothly from one to the next. Consider the following suggestions; add, change, or rearrange to obtain the best flow.

Journal. Use this section to include meaningful experiences and daily thoughts on spirituality, Wicca, divinity, and magick. This is also a perfect space to create poetry, art, and dream notes.

Goddess and God. Utilize this section for deity myths, stories, invocations, prayers, and guided meditations.

Circle Casting. Record your personal circle casting (see chapter Six on creating one). Include a diagram of your altar layout, quick ritual checklist, and tool information.

Rituals. Enclose rituals for the Sabbats, Full Moons, as well as a multipurpose consecration rite and an altar devotion format.

Correspondences. Space for all your material on magick, timing, candle colors, as well as properties of herbs, oils, incense, etc.

Spells. In this area, keep a record of the magick you've cast and include your favorite spells.

Additional suggested items to enclose in your Book of Shadows:

> Book blessing
> Story on how you came to Wicca
> Personal stats: your Craft name, birthday, astrological sign, etc.
> Thoughts and reflections on magick
> Full poetic version of the Wiccan Rede
> Ritual and spell sheet (see example, on the next page)

Looking to save time? Photocopy rituals or information-filled pages from your favorite Wicca books (such as the Altar Blessing Ritual in chapter Three). Hole-punch and place in your Book of Shadows for easy access. Remember to write down the book's title, author, and page number on the back for future reference.

After you've crafted your Book of Shadows, write your own blessing ritual. To gain the most benefit from the Book of Shadows, try to write in it often. If your schedule doesn't allow for writing every day, consistently writing once a week will more than suffice. May your book become a beautiful reflection of your magical journey. Enjoy!

Ritual and Spell Sheet

RITUAL/SPELL NAME	PURPOSE	DATE
1.		
2.		
3.		
4.		
5.		
6.		
7.		
8.		
9.		
10.		
11.		
12.		
13.		
14.		
15.		
16.		
17.		
18.		
19.		
20.		

Divination

Divination is the magical art of discovering unanswered questions pertaining to the past, present, or future. Using the psychic mind along with a learned skill and aid of the Goddess and God, divination becomes a tool used to obtain insight and guidance. Falsely portrayed as fortune-telling, the tarot, runes, and other methods enable us to learn possible outcomes and reveal hidden choices. It is a process of being receptive to the energies within and using them to take a step in the right direction. The messages provided from using divination tools aren't set in stone and can be changed by taking a different course of action. Some Wiccans use divination; others do not. It is a completely optional practice. Those who do practice this art utilize specific implements or objects to:

- Make day to day choices

- Gain further understanding of a particular situation or circumstance

- Read for others to help them gain insight into their life

- Heighten awareness of the intuitive forces and psychic mind

- Determine if magick should be worked or put on hold till another time

There aren't strict rules in regard to divination practice so honor your natural ethics. As a word of advice, don't take the results too seriously—sometimes a reading can be wrong. Follow your intuition when you feel off course. In this section I have included a description of several of the more popular methods used and a few tips on caring for these divination tools. Although not discussed in this section, other divination techniques include: numerology, dowsing, reading tea leaves, numerology, and I Ching.

A **tarot** deck is comprised of seventy-eight illustrated cards, which are divided into two sets: twenty-two Major Arcana and fifty-six Minor Arcana. The Major cards represent significant spiritual issues, phases, changes and challenges. The Minor Arcana represents everyday life situations, relationships, finances, etc. The Minor cards are broken down further into suits: Pentacles, Wands, Cups, and Swords. Some decks use alternative phrases such as Coins instead of Pentacles or Staves in place of Wands, however they still have the same meanings. The four suits also relate to the elements. Pentacles are linked to earth; Wands are associated with fire; Cups correspond to water; and Swords correlate with air. To utilize the tarot, the deck is shuffled and cards are laid out into a predetermined spread. One by one, each card is revealed and the meaning is determined by its specific placement and individual symbolism.

Scrying is the art of gazing at an object's surface, settling the mind and allowing pictures to form in your third eye (brow Chakra). Common tools used for scrying are a crystal sphere, darkened mirror, water-filled cauldron, or bowl. This vision induced process is often done by candlelight; afterward, symbols received are recorded and interpreted.

Palmistry is the divination art of reading hands. Many know that a palmist looks at the unique lines, but they also consider overall size, shape, and length of a hand. Finger shape and length also come into play. Once each of these key elements are assessed and consulted the hand can reveal life circumstances, personality traits, and even the future!

Runes are a set of twenty-five symbols used in both magick and divination. In this case, runes come in two forms: illustrated on cards (much like a tarot deck) and inscribed on individual stones (or wooden/clay tablets). The latter is more popular because of the ability and ease of crafting a set for oneself. Rune sets are Norse in origin, representing different aspects of life such as home, work, money, as well as spiritual/emotional concerns like love, creativity, or fear. Using this divination system is similar to that of tarot—read them via a specific spread or layout. Alternatively, one rune pulled can help answer a specific question or address a looming issue.

Care for Divination Tools

- When you just receive a new divination tool, consecrate the item to insure protection from negative energies.

- Keep in the same place, preferably in an altar box (or basket) when not in use.

- Handle and use the tool continuously to forge a connection of energy.

- Meditate before use and ask for the Goddess and God to bless your reading with accuracy.

- When you complete a reading, write a few brief sentences on your experience. Record your question, clarity of response, and how the answer you received impacted your initial perception.

❦ From Gwinevere's Book of Shadows

October 31, 2001—Age 17

During my Samhain ritual I burned sage and used my new pendulum. I asked what path my writing career will take and other queries about my life's direction. Performing divination is insightful especially on Samhain when the gates to the other realms are open. I often find my psychic awareness and intuition are heightened around this time.

TWO

The Good Wiccan

What makes a good Wiccan? The answer might surprise you. Being a good Wiccan isn't about doing everything flawless or correct the first time. In this religion no one expects perfection. The answer doesn't have to do with external elements, the amount of altar tools you have, number of books read, or years of practice accumulated. Being a good Wiccan means honoring yourself, living ethically, and opening your mind, body, and soul to the universe and her messages.

The title of this chapter is a play on words. Like Glenda asked Dorothy in *The Wizard of Oz*, Are you a good witch or a bad witch? She should have asked if her goal was to help or hinder. Specific codes of conduct attempt to guide Wiccans on a firm moral path. Since these ethics don't go into detail dissecting every possible situation that we might encounter in our daily lives, the phrase *up to individual interpretation* often follows. It is not easy being left to negotiate the details, but it's necessary for your personal and spiritual development. These guidelines aren't meant to restrict your life; they are for your benefit not just as a Wiccan but also as a person, and to bring meaning to your craft.

I think Wicca has opened my eyes and mind. I feel more deeply and I am more open toward my feelings.
—LUNA, AGE 16, FINLAND

The Wiccan Rede

Often when we are defining our beliefs for those who don't know about the Wiccan religion, we relay our concept of deity, describe magick and holidays, but most of all we seek to explain Wiccan ethics. Our Rede, *An ye harm none,* is the foundation of Wicca. It is one small phrase with powerful and breathtaking meaning. Despite all the different traditions and eclectic ways, it is this rule that unites us.

My path has given me a sense of self-empowerment. By practicing my spirituality, I am able to feel in charge of my life.
—PYTHO, AGE 14, MILAN, ITALY

When a person identifies themselves as a Wiccan this label tells me that they try to live their life honestly, following intuition and moral guidelines. The Wiccan Rede clarifies to every practitioner that they should walk the path morally and ethically, allowing no room for deviation. Specific practices may vary greatly but Wiccans honoring the Rede is an ever strengthening, uniting, and bonding thread. In full length the Wiccan Rede is a beautiful poem, detailing ritual, deity and specific ways of conduct. Since "The Rede of the Wiccae" submitted by Lady Gwen Thompson was first published in *Green Egg Magazine,* several Wiccan traditions have instituted their own version. A second, equally popular Rede is Doreen Valiente's "Witch's Creed," published in *Witchcraft for Tomorrow.* The latter creed is a staple within the Gardnerian Tradition. Recently many books and websites have gone into great detail, dissecting the meaning of the Wiccan Rede verse by verse. I choose to look at the whole picture and overall message. If you are confused or taken aback by the many versions, put aside the fancy language and ritualistic references because every Rede boils down to one thing: harm none.

> *I do not actively practice the Wiccan Rede in its common form, though I do consider my spiritual path to be influenced by the Golden Rule, "Do unto others as you would have them do unto you."*
> —GEDE, AGE 15, QUEENSLAND, AUSTRALIA

I admit, *harm none* is a phrase casually thrown around when attempting to define our ethics. However, upon careful reflection I found myself asking, what exactly does this mean? Why use the word *none* instead of something like *anyone* or *any person*? I came upon the realization that there is a deeper meaning behind the phrase. Since we all interpret things differently, I may not be able to give you a complete answer that will satisfy your own beliefs, but I'll share a definition that I personally use: Harm none means doing your very best to refrain from hurting anyone (including yourself) physically, mentally, or emotionally. In my mind it goes without saying that animals—both family pets and wildlife—should never be purposefully hurt either. Cruelty to animals is awful and has no place in Wicca.

The correlation between Witchcraft and specific outlined ethics is lacking. Unlike Wicca, the path of Witchcraft isn't well defined. People are still debating if Witchcraft should even be viewed as a religion! Some believe this vagueness is a positive, because it doesn't restrain practitioners in any way. Others see it more negatively, believing there should be clear rules of conduct. Regardless, when you hear a person refer to oneself as a "Wiccan," you can safely assume they respect the Rede to the best of their ability.

I believe the Wiccan Rede is a law against malicious harm. The key idea is to respect life and find a balance.
—ARIAWN, AGE 19, OHIO, USA

❧ From Gwinevere's Book of Shadows

May 28, 1999—Age 14

Sometimes I wonder if everyone in the world followed the idea of harm none, how different things might be. Everything would change.

I believe that the Wiccan Rede is more like a poem than a law; decisions must be made with sense and heart.

—LUNA, AGE 16, FINLAND

I consider equating the Rede with other popular religious and spiritual creeds. This reinforces that despite the difference of belief there is a common element that all faith systems generally share: We should treat each other kindly and in respect of the sacred.

—GEDE, AGE 15, QUEENSLAND, AUSTRALIA

The Rule of Three

The Rule of Three (also referred to as the Threefold Law) is an extension of the Wiccan Rede. At its core the Rule of Three's message is a Karmic warning: What energy you send out and actions you take will eventually return threefold. This concept isn't new. In fact, the expression "Do unto others as you would have them do unto you" is hundreds of years old. Wiccans just put an extra spin on it. Your energy, positive or negative, returns back to you at some point within this lifetime but three times as powerful. The universe figures out how and when. We control the aspect of why.

I don't believe Karma is meant to hurt anyone who is a good person or prevent us from living our lives to the fullest. The purpose is to be aware of even the littlest negative action. For example stealing a book seems petty in the grand scheme of things, but just knowing the universe is keeping an eye out makes a person think twice. The Rede establishes ethical guidelines and the Rule of Three makes you aware of the possible consequences.

❧ From Gwinevere's Book of Shadows

July 14, 1999—Age 14

It wasn't until recently that I started considering the Rule of Three outside of any magical context. What if everything I put out into the world returns back to me at some point? All my good would create positives, and my other not-so-good actions would return with negative influences. I feel as if this piece of information is a guide to my future. Live positive, get positive. Considering how much energy it takes to be rude and hurtful, why should I bother? There are more benefits to staying on a good path.

I believe in the scientific and metaphysical law of "action and re-action": that all actions bear consequence dependent upon the nature of the initial action.

—GEDE, AGE 15, QUEENSLAND, AUSTRALIA

Magick & Ethics

I can't fully grasp why some Wiccans think magick spells give our craft a bad name. It is true, the media tends to focus on spells and some beginners are blind to the fact that there is a religion behind magick. However, that is no excuse to say snobby things like "Being Wiccan is more than lighting a candle and chanting words." Magick is beautiful. We need to embrace its power and majesty, not shove it in the corner where dust gathers!

Magick is a part of us, a part of this path, to be respected and used whenever your inner compass suggests. With that said, let's talk about the responsibility of magick. If you've been practicing for a while now, you probably have a feeling for what situations are best to use magickal assistance and which ones should be left to mundane means and fixes. For newer Wiccans, listen up, its time to go over a few magical guidelines.

> *I stay away from spells that would alter someone's free will or emotions, as those are two things I believe are sacred and should not be tampered with.*
> —CHIRON NIGHTWOLF, AGE 16, GEORGIA, USA

POSITIVE VS. NEGATIVE

Part of making magick work is focusing on the desired outcome. A person's desire also connects with their intent. Before I start writing a spell I ask myself, what is my exact need and desire? I think of the goal and carefully consider the Wiccan Rede. I'll stop writing if I feel my spell might hurt or manipulate another person. Therefore, I consciously become aware of my intent.

I don't use the labels "white witchcraft" or "black magick" because intent can't be color-coded. Instead, I use the concepts of positive versus negative. Positive spells, like ones for healing or protection bring about good, helpful endings. Negative spells like hexing, purposefully use magick to harm or control. Most times, it's easy to identify the intent. If the task proves to be a challenge, try your best and deliberate with the Rede in mind.

> *I only cast spells or work with magick to achieve an end when I feel it is completely necessary and after I have attempted other ways and methods.*
> —GEDE, AGE 15, QUEENSLAND, AUSTRALIA

CASTING SPELLS WHEN OTHERS ARE INVOLVED

When a family member or friend approaches you with a spell request, the situation can at times feel uncomfortable. I can't tell you what to do, but I can provide several handy tips.

1. First, be honest. If you don't feel like you have enough experience, say so! Kindly express, "I'd like to keep learning about magick before I venture into casting spells for other people." Alternatively, encourage this person to cast the spell on their own. If that is not an option, offer to cast it together. This way you'll help their situation, meanwhile they have the opportunity to experience a part of your path.

2. Take some time to think about their request—they want *you* to cast *their* spell for *them*. How do you feel about this? Is the cause worthy? Are they asking you to prove that your magick is real? Do they respect you or do you feel used? Will the spell interfere with your personal morals or Wiccan ethics?

3. Learn to say no. One spell with a real need is fine. Five spell requests in a limited time period is asking too

much! Turn them down in a polite yet firm way, then try to offer alternatives (i.e., confronting the situation in a nonmagical way, prayer or meditation) so they don't go away empty-handed.

4. There may be other occasions when you'll see someone in need and want to help. For example, your best friend just went through a harsh breakup. It's natural to turn to magick as a means of support. However, think for a moment about his or her needs. What if they don't really *need* a spell, just someone to talk to? Often, there are ways to help that don't include magick.

I have used healing magic for a friend before. I was in a small group, and the overall atmosphere was warm, comfortable, and loving. Though the room was dim, we all saw a bright light, and felt the presence of the Goddess as we asked her to help our friend in her time of need. It was truly a memorable experience.
—CHIRON NIGHTWOLF, AGE 16, GEORGIA, USA

Let's look at another example. A family member caught a cold and you want to come to the rescue. You make them soup, and find the TV remote for them in the sofa cushions, but you want to do more. A healing spell could send positive, loving vibrations their way. Before you cast one, keep in mind the Wiccan Rede. "Harm none" includes any work that interferes with another's free will. To make sure it's okay to go ahead with the spell, politely ask your loved one for their permission. Listen to their answer, no matter the reply. Despite good intentions, some people don't want any spells cast on their behalf. In these cases, prayer is a great alternative. Quiet your mind and speak to the Goddess and God. Ask for their assistance and then leave it in the hands of divinity.

LOVE SPELLS

The topic of love spells is an important subject matter. *Please read this part carefully.* I believe that focusing on a particular person to get them to fall in love with you, breaking up a relation-

---

🌿 From Gwinevere's Book of Shadows

April 2, 2001—Age 16

There is a sensitivity needed when working spells for others. A family member or friend is investing trust, hoping to attain some needed task healing, protection, or the deep desire to feel loved. I do what I can, not just with magick but moral support. I feel like part of my life as a Wiccan is to help others in whatever way I am able to: a hug, a smile, an open mind, to be a trusted ally in this harsh world.

✤ From Gwinevere's Book of Shadows

June 4, 2003—Age 18

I created and cast a "warrior spell" for a friend of mine. The magical purpose was to improve inner strength, conviction, and confidence. Normally, I connect with my personal energy through my third eye (I feel it pulsate) but this time, it was through my heart. It beat faster and felt full and warm.

ship, or altering someone's emotions for your benefit are all violations of the Wiccan Rede, intrude on free will, and create bad Karma that will eventually return.

Using a "person-specific" love spell to manipulate another's feelings is never a good idea. Why? Because love is supposed to come naturally. It is a deep spiritual connection that voluntarily develops between two people—not a process to mess around with.

Are there other kinds of love spells that are okay to cast? Yes! There are plenty of alternatives to those creepy zombie love spells. Consider the following magick ideas to help fill your heart and benefit your spirit:

- *Improved Self-Love.* Embrace your inner power and people will naturally be drawn to your confidence.

- *Right Person, Right Now.* You're not looking for marriage or a soul mate; you just want a fun, smart, sensitive person right now!

- *Invite Love.* Name qualities you're looking for in a guy or young woman and "invite" them into your life.

A general spell to attract more love, to feel love, or express love is just fine.
—ARIAWN, AGE 19, OHIO, USA

If you're ever stuck wondering, "Is this spell okay to cast?" ask yourself the following questions and you'll have your answer!

1. Would I mind if this spell were cast on me?

2. Am I willing to take the responsibility of my actions?

3. By working this spell am I going to harm anyone or intrude on someone's free will?

Finally, if you're still undecided and questioning the spell's end result, don't cast it! It is better to err on the side of caution.

Wiccan Rules and Everyday Life

Many beginners see the Rede and Rule of Three only as magical guidelines, but these rules cover so much more. They are ethics for everyday life! The tricky part is incorporating a basic statement of "harm none" into daily situations. One key idea is to be aware of your actions. If you're feeling upset about something you've said or done, it's probably an indication of negative actions. Then it's up to you to make the situation right.

Don't let this task overwhelm you. Little by little, you'll come to incorporate the Rede within your life. Also be aware that even when your internal conflict ends, other Wiccans might chime in and disagree. Live your path the way you see fit. Other people will always have their opinions but it's your practice!

One topic that stirs up heated debates is vegetarianism. It's been said that being a vegetarian is part of honoring the Rede. I completely understand the goal but, in my mind it's a lifestyle choice and one option I've decided not to take part in. There are many Wiccans who recognize that vegetarianism isn't right for everyone but some can't get past their particular interpretation of the Rede and may try to use seniority or guilt as weapons. Stand tall in your choice, whichever that may be.

> *The Wiccan Rede urges us to evaluate and consider our actions before we commit to the consequences.*
> —GEDE, AGE 15, QUEENSLAND, AUSTRALIA

> *Wicca has taught me many things about power—not over people, but over my life. I have learned that I am the only person responsible for my actions, accomplishments, and faults.*
> —ANUBIS RAINHAWK, AGE 15, CALIFORNIA, USA

Charting Your Path

Throughout this chapter we've analyzed Wiccan rules and guidelines. These ideas mold together and form basic Wiccan structure. It is up to you to build and shape your spiritual journey on top of this foundation. Your personal path won't be mapped out for you, so you'll have to chart it yourself. Remember, when you're stuck, tap into the power of your intuition for meaningful guidance.

The following questions are a suggested starting point. Take as much time as you need to answer them. It does not matter if you choose to gradually address them over several days or complete them within a few minutes. Record the answers in your Book of Shadows.

What initially sparked your interest to research this path?

Describe any positive changes that Wicca has bought to your life.

Complete the following sentence: Being Wiccan means:

Define in your own words the term harm none.

Do you see yourself as a solitary practitioner for years down the line or do you have a deep interest in working with others as an organized group or coven?

What term(s) do you like best when defining your own path?

What life passions and practices, magical or mundane, fulfill you?

Do you feel naturally psychic or intuitive? Are you interested in expanding or building upon your abilities?

What does magick practice mean to you on a deep, personal level?

Do you feel your path is lacking in any way? If so, explain what feelings or practices you desire to add.

Circle any of the following that you have an interest in and write a quick sentence about why they appeal to you. Healing, Moon Work, Divination, Goddess Research, The Elements, Herbalism/Natural Magick, etc.

What feelings do you have in regard to the practice of working skyclad (in the nude)?

Do you want to honor or focus on deities from any specific pantheon (e.g., Celtic, Egyptian, or Norse gods and goddesses)?

What are your thoughts on reincarnation?

Do you have any past-life memories?

If one day you decided to make a life union with another person, will you have a Wiccan handfasting or traditional wedding?

Are there any Wiccan practices that you disagree with and don't want to incorporate within your path?

In the future, do you see yourself teaching Wicca to others?

Do you have any methods or ways of practice you'd like to master, such as tarot, candle magick, or prolonged mediation?

When you picture yourself as a Wiccan years down the line, what do you see?

❧ From Gwinevere's Book of Shadows

May 17, 2003—Age 18

It took the longest time for me to stop doubting my practice. The funny thing is my doubts were always about myself and my abilities, never "Is this path correct for me?" It was like once I knew I was Wiccan, I never teetered in my decision. For years I doubted if I were a good Wiccan, if I stood up to the ideal image. Even after writing books and having my website, I am not the "perfect Wiccan." You know what, I don't want to be, because then I'd have to worry about staying perfect. I am a Wiccan, not a bad one, not a perfect one, but nonetheless a Wiccan.

Even with the completion of these questions, it's important to realize that your journey can't always be mapped out point to point. As an intermediate practitioner it will be up to you to continuously mold and shape your own path.

I know at times Wicca may feel overwhelming, like you're being pulled in different directions. My advice to you is to try to take each day one at a time, think positively, follow your intuition, and use Wiccan ethics as your compass. Have patience; slowly skills will develop and information will sink in. You don't need to memorize hundreds of deities' names or whole books of herbal correspondences.

Sometimes you'll miss a Sabbat or skip a Full Moon ritual and that is all right! The criteria for a "good Wiccan" isn't perfect attendance, it's what you feel inside and how you choose to live your path—honestly and ethically.

THREE

The Goddess and God

Honoring divinity is a central practice of the Wiccan faith. Within this chapter you'll find information on The Goddess and God, how to establish a connection with them as well as ritual invocations and everyday prayers.

History

Ancient Goddess worship is evident through paleolithic art. Statues like Venus of Willendorf (a female figure with full belly and breasts) were deliberately sculpted to depict life-producing "fertility" icons. As cultures evolved, deity worship became more detailed. Creation myths were used to explain the beginning of Earth and human life. Many creation stories are beautiful, dramatic tales that introduce a collection of deities called a *pantheon*.

Some ancient cultures even have creation myths that begin with a female essence, a "creatrix," life-initiating mother of the gods. Two great examples are the Finnish Luonnotar and Greek Gaia. Egyptian's Neith and Babylonian's Tiamat are also primordial mother Goddesses, but can't take sole responsibility as they had male deity assistance.

For modern-day Goddess worshipers, these bits of history help validate our belief. The Goddess exists; she always has. Occasionally, Wicca is called a "fertility religion." This means several things. First, the understanding that the Goddess breathes life into all things; second, that women like the Goddess are able to create life; and third, the bounty of the Earth shows us that we can bring change and creativity into the world, producing abundant and fruitful results.

The impact of Goddess belief is far-reaching and consistently evolving.

Wiccan View

Many practitioners acknowledge a supreme divine power referred to as The One or The All. This life energy is the ultimate source of all things. However, it is so unknowable and beyond deep comprehension that Wiccans break down this essence into two forms, the Goddess and God. They are dual, two halves of a whole and work as complementary equals. The Goddess and God are seen as warm and loving, caring and compassionate. We can find them not in a distant unreachable heaven, but in nature and deep within ourselves. They are "omnipresent," existing everywhere at the same time.

We give them names, faces and attributes in order to envision their love and connect with their power. There is a saying in Wicca: "All Gods are one God." This means that no matter the aspect you reach out to Cernunnos, Gwydion, Green Man, you'll still be communing with the core masculine deity. This same principle applies to the Goddess. She is multifaceted and viewed differently by various cultures, but in the end all prayers lead to Her.

Divinity encompasses the role of protector, nurturer, and teacher. They watch over, guide, help, send obstacles to make us stronger, and release hope to help us carry on. Their message is one of love not hate, peace not war. The Goddess doesn't judge by color or gender; the God shows us to value the life cycle. All acts of love are Her ritual, and He wants you to work with your natural gifts and grab hold of your true potential. They have a lot to show us and we have a lot to learn. Wiccans who open themselves to the Goddess and God find the most powerful magick of all—a welcoming embrace.

✤ From Gwinevere's Book of Shadows

September 24, 1999—Age 15

I don't admit it often, but I think about the God every day. I find it so easy to relate to the Goddess, but the God is like a puzzle I am still trying to figure out. Who is he? Does he watch over us? When I picture him I see different things . . . a strong warrior in battle gear fighting to protect humankind, a magician making potions, a smiling, white-bearded man. Then concepts come to mind: the sound of a hearty laugh, a comforting embrace, the warm sun, a forest that goes deeper and deeper.

The Goddess is not purely feminine and the God is not purely masculine. If you look at the yin-yang symbol, you see that both sides have each other, but would be incomplete without the other. Like the yin-yang symbol, both God and Goddess are part of a greater whole called the Great Spirit or the Brahman. When you call upon one, you are, in essence, calling both.
—ANUBIS RAINHAWK, AGE 15, CALIFORNIA, USA

If I need strength, I often ask the God to help and if I need to be caring and wise, I ask the Goddess.
—LUNA, AGE 16, FINLAND

Connect with Divinity

When I first began researching Wicca, I asked a more experienced practitioner a question that had been on my mind: Do Wiccans have churches or temples? The person replied, "The Earth is my church." Deep inside something stirred. I realized to connect with Mother Earth, I should look to her life source—nature. A building is only a structure, but the green lands are alive with divine energy! You don't have to be in the middle of a forest to understand nature; you can observe it by partaking in an evening walk as the sun sets and moon rises or opening a window during spring cleaning to hear the birds chirp.

As time progressed I discovered that there are even more ways to connect with divinity. Reading ancient myths from various cultures can give you a more detailed understanding of specific gods and goddesses. Each pantheon has its own complex group of deities, complete with stories and ruling aspects. Whether you delve into artistic Greeks, heroic Norse, mystical

Egyptians, or the strong-willed Celtic, you'll find something that speaks to your spirit.

> *When I connect, I feel this sense of ultimate peace. There is energy, power, and joy but most of all, unconditional love. I am able to see myself and my place within the universe, and I feel more whole after pausing to make a connection.*
> —ARIAWN, AGE 19, OHIO, USA

Enrich yourself in the Goddess's journey by following her monthly moon cycle, and learn the Gods story by participating in Sabbat rituals throughout the wheel of the year. Truly engaging in their cyclic rituals makes all the difference!

Prayer is also a meaningful way to connect with divinity. In the back of this chapter, I've enclosed prayers for self-love, financial support, guidance, and protection. Use them as starting points and learn to create your own spiritual petitions.

Other ways to attune with the Goddess and God include altar devotions, writing poems, letters, or invocations, and creating special rituals in their honor.

❧ From Gwinevere's Book of Shadows

May 9, 2002—Age 17

One of the best ways I am able to connect with the higher powers is through consistent communication. Some nights, I pray to the Goddess and God as I lie in bed. I ask them to protect and guide me. Or I'll sit at my altar, candles lit and just talk. I'll tell them my problems, invite any solutions they may have. The point isn't to hear the voice of divinity come down and answer back, but to acknowledge their presence in my life.

I connect with the higher powers daily, when I'm doing my daily meditation. I feel they give me power and I feel a nice, tickling sensation. I feel energized and refreshed.
LUNA, AGE 16, FINLAND

The Triple Goddess

The Triple Goddess is a theme found in Wicca that represents the Lady in her three forms: Maiden, Mother, and Crone. Each aspect relates to points in the lunar cycle and has specific attributes and energies. The Triple Goddess symbol is made up of two crescents snuggling each side of a full moon. Although many Goddesses fall into one of these three classifications, some female deities will not. This is because the Triple Goddess concept is rather new. We cannot force ancient pantheons to fit into our organized idea of the Goddess. Here is a basic overview of the Triple Goddess construct. I deeply encourage you to further research the idea if you feel it will aid your understanding of the Goddess.

MAIDEN (NEW AND WAXING MOON)
Youthful/sister phase of the Goddess personified by deities such as Artemis, Hebe, Ostara, Persephone, Kore. Rules: beginnings, new growth, inspiration.

MOTHER (FULL MOON)
Creator/nurturing phase of the Goddess personified by deities such as Demeter, Ceres, Frigg, Hera, Selene. Rules: psychic awareness, intuition, fruitfulness, healing, protection.

CRONE (DARK AND WANING MOON)
Sage/grandmother phase of the Goddess personified by deities such as Cailleagh, Cerridwen, and Hecate. Rules: divination, spirituality, wisdom.

❧ From Gwinevere's Book of Shadows

June 1, 2003—Age 18

I love the concept of the Triple Goddess. She is everything all at once, young, old, maternal—every aspect of life wisdom is located in her essence. She is a powerhouse Goddess who can whisper or roar.

Patron Deities

Once you've become acclimated to the concept of both a Goddess and God you may decide to go one step further and forge a working relationship with their specific aspects. Taking on a patron Goddess and God is optional, but some practitioners find deeper bonds and fulfilment by partaking in this practice. Deciding to work with one specific Goddess and God continuously is an important decision and should be made after much forethought and deliberation. You're going to position them to be the focus of your Wiccan faith.

Since each person is unique, various deities will call to different people. How can you select your patron Goddess and God? There are several methods to establish this link and even further ways to continue your connection.

After reading up on pantheons that you're drawn to, look deeper into deities that stood out in your mind. Do any of the

Gods or Goddess rule over aspects you're seeking to attain in your life, such as love, protection, guidance, or wisdom? Do you keep coming across a certain Goddess name over and over even when you aren't specifically pursuing her? Are there any Gods who are in sync with your own character, energy, or creative skills? If you're stuck, think of a deity concept such as lunar goddess or earthly god, then seek out those deities who rule over such aspects.

Next, learn their story: Who are their consorts, allies, family? Feel their energy, meditate while chanting their name. If you're starting to feel a good harmony then you're on the right track. Although it's often recommended that your patron Goddess and God come from the same pantheon it is acceptable to choose them from two different cultures. However, if you're sensing that their energies aren't compatible, you may have to rethink your decision.

Continue to familiarize yourself with these potential patron deities. There is no set time limit in this process. Once you've started to develop a positive rapport and you feel ready to take the next step, set aside several days to write a personal ritual in their names. Let the words come from your heart, and perform it with meaning. Dedicate yourself as a follower of their ways.

Once you've established a spiritual kinship, you'll want to continuously pay tribute and work with these deities. Here are several suggestions:

- Invite them each time you cast a circle.

- Create or purchase statues to represent your patron Goddess and God.

- Use colors linked to them on your altar in the form of an altar cloth, candles, or candleholders.

- Write poems detailing their myth.

- Make incense/oil blends with herbs and scents that connect with your deities.

- Incorporate symbols or objects of significance to them on your altar.

- Research their symbolic animals, especially if the Goddess and God are viewed in those alternate forms.

- Pray to them when you seek guidance.

- Find out if there were ancient festivals held in their honor. Hold a special ceremony around that time in honor.

I have a calling from Erzulie-Dantor and Ogoun. Through a personal experience involving the Black Madonna and my own painting, I was able to connect Erzulie to my life. And with her came Ogoun. These two deities are from the vodou pantheon and have a more "active" than passive energy in them. I believe these deities called me to help establish the pause in life. Things were never stagnant when I started invoking them, and although some trials were difficult, they were memorable.
—PYTHO, AGE 14, MILAN, ITALY

Preference Debate

The subtle dynamics of Wiccan practice changes from person to person. We each add nuances to our craft, personalizing the faith so it fits into our lives. One of these alterations is usually a result of the way we work with, imagine, and pay respect to divinity.

Even though Wicca is based on balance and duality, it is not uncommon for practitioners to put an emphasis on the Goddess. Whether you agree with this occurrence or not, it is important to see both sides of the coin. What is the motivation behind uplifting the Goddess and subtracting or demoting the God? What negative impacts could occur as a result of this action? Here you'll find two distinct points of view, along with my personal notes and experiences.

Wiccans who focus primarily or exclusively on the Goddess have several valid reasons. Many times practitioners come from monotheistic Yahweh-centered belief systems, religions that suggest an all-powerful singular male god. This can be disenfranchising to women who want to honor a deity they can actually relate to. The Goddess has energy that is nurturing, warm, and comforting. Even though she has her occasional dark side, (think of Mother Nature in full fury: hurricanes, tornadoes, etc.) she isn't supposed to be feared; instead she is to be revered! The Goddess represents freedom, love, and the essence of life.

> *I was drawn to Kali for many reasons. For one thing, her appearance alone is extremely profound and inspiring. Kali's skin color represents a lack of color, conveying her as the ultimate reality. She is the Holy Mother, with two hands she creates, and with two hands she destroys.*
> —ANUBIS RAINHAWK, AGE 15, CALIFORNIA, USA

Aside from religion, the consistent struggle to emerge from a patriarchal society (male-dominant beliefs or rule) motives the elevation of a feminine deity. It's about taking a stand, saying, "She exists, believe it. Women are the human embodiment of the Great Goddess, you cannot deny us." I am sure there are a dozen other reasons for focusing on the Goddess but all roads come to one conclusion: She gives us empowerment.

On the flip side, the argument can be made that only paying homage to the Goddess puts the idea of balance in jeopardy. What about male Wiccans seeking a deity they can relate to? Are we then going against nature itself, which is comprised of both male and female creatures? The wheel of the myth would have to be rewritten, taken out or demoting the God's role. Is it fair to take parts of Wicca you like and ignore the parts you don't want to see?

After several years of practice I am still learning about the God and seeking to understand him. What I do know is that in my practice he may not play center stage, but his role is needed. The Goddess and God are intertwined, two parts of a whole. His spark, fire, passion, and zest complement her calmness. He is the force that pushes me forward with my goals, the protector and warrior who guides me every day. He is the son and partner of the Goddess. I come in contact with his energy as the wheel turns with each Sabbat.

Yet, the Goddess is my sister, and advisor. She is like me: feminine. I relate to her on a deeper level that I haven't reached with the God. A part of me is still seeking to understand him and his permanent role in my life. What I do know is that I am trying, and that is what matters and what counts. My practice consistently lends new ways to see them both, which is something I can truly embrace.

To learn more about Goddess-focused practitioners, read up on Dianic or Feminist traditions. Authors such as Starhawk, Patricia Monaghan, and M. J. Abadie offer literary sources in regard to Goddess reverence.

> I place a slight preference on the Goddess mostly in my vernacular and not in my actual worship. Oftentimes I will refer to the Goddess as a way to distinguish between Yahweh-centered belief systems and other religions.
> —ARIAWN, AGE 19, OHIO, USA

I believe there should be more books on the God of the Wiccan religion. There are very few texts that refer to the Lord and countless that emphasize the Lady. This is because so many people have lost that sense of balance and totally demoted the Horned God.
—PYTHO, AGE 14, MILAN, ITALY

I see the Goddess and the God as equal entities, but I find myself looking to the Goddess for help more than the God. I believe I do this because all my life, I have not had a "father" in my life. I find it much easier to put faith and trust in the Goddess as a Mother.
—CHIRON NIGHTWOLF, AGE 16, GEORGIA, USA

My Favorite Invocations and Prayers

Lunar Goddess Invocation
*To you I call, midnight enchantress,
send down your love in silver stream,
release you silken charm through lunar beam
mystical Goddess of the moon, to your image I now face
and ask that you enter my circle, this sacred space.*

Maiden Goddess Invocation
*Maiden of spring, I call to you
whose birdsong echos in field of growing wheat
tasting bitter tart and yet honey sweet
where cream butterflies and bumblebees
dance by smiling soft daisies
Maiden of floral delight
youthful smile, cheeks rosy bright
I call to you, young natured one
she who is vernal
blessed and eternal*

Moon Goddess Invocation
Goddess of the Moon
cyclic, eternal, sacred, and free
Artemis, Ishtar, Aradia, and Selene
I invite thee, ancient beauty
I send my call in prayer and praise
seeking your presence and protective ways
blessed I shall be in your divine light
within my circle this darkened night.

Freya Invocation
Freya, fair one
Goddess of love and sorcery
who rides cat-drawn chariot
and sheds amber tears
mistress of sexuality
spirit of fertility
Freya, fair one
I call upon you!

Triple Goddess Invocation

Triple Goddess of Blessed Cycles
O'Maiden who is sisterly
O'Mother who is nurturing
O'Crone who is saged
I invoke thee
to draw down your love
to seek your presence
please lend your power
be here in sacred space.

Isis Invocation

Isis, winged Goddess of Creation
Lady of ten thousand names
whose power and compassion
heals and protects
beautiful Egyptian Goddess
Isis, I invoke you
with respect and reverence
descend I ask
bare witness to this mystical rite.

God Invocation

O'God, I invite you to my circle
Mythical warrior, father of time
he who is both harvest and wine
Guardian of the fall and mysteries
keeper of wind and dark trembling sea
I invite you to my circle
please be here!

Green Man Invocation
Holly, Oak, Mistletoe, Thistle
He who is darkened forest
Green Man with face of leaves and woven branch
found deep in earthen hills
by cascading ivy vines
in bark of tallest trees
male spirit of nature
I invoke He who is . . .
Green Man, my lord.

Sun God Invocation
O'Lord of Sun
my shinning one
who's known by many names
Bel, Lugh, Helios
I call to you
please bear witness to this sacred rite
bring down your silken solar light
be here with me.

Gwydion Invocation

Celtic Gwydion
weaver of magick, wise warrior-God
please join my sacred space
bring with you the winds of change I seek
for you are the prince of air, helper of humankind
bard of northern wales
legendary enchanter
with open hear
I welcome you, Gwydion!

Cernunnos Invocation

Cernunnos, horned one
master of woodland animals
I call to you
deity of power and strength
who guards the underworld gates
spinner of cycles
birth, life, death
earthly, phallic
Cernunnos
I call to you!

Horus Invocation

Horus, magical child
falcon God, ruler of vast horizon
I speak to thee and ask for your guiding watch
Egyptian lord, young one
I invoke you with love and respect

Deity Call

I call to you with child voice
unshakable love
breathless spirit

I draw upon your divine strength
boundless compassion
brightest blessings

I invite your essence
Lord and Lady
come soft as windfeather
bring hope-filled message
stay for rite and spell
I invite you, my divine ones.

Fall Harvest Prayer

Earth Mother, Ceres, Demeter, Modron
She who is gentle and giving
I offer thanks for this feast of plenty and gifts of sustenance
fertile enchantress
I am grateful for your bountiful harvest spell!

Prayer for Financial Support

Lakshmi, she who rides upon lotus flower
Hindu Goddess of abundance and beauty
I pray to you upon this night and ask for your assistance
Please bless my family with good fortune and prosperity
Lakshmi, thank you.

Prayer for Self-Love

Hathor, compassionate Goddess
I pray to you, gift me beauty

true loveliness inside and out
bless me with empowerment
awaken my inner jewel of passion and pleasure
grant me the vision of sacred self-love.

Prayer for Guidance
Athena, Greek warrior Goddess of wisdom
I pray to you for guidance
please help me overcome towering obstacles in my way
bless me with your kind strength and conviction
lend sage advice and instill courage during this time of need.

Healing Prayer
Great Celtic Brigid
keeper of the sacred flame
I pray to you Threefold Goddess
please aid me
send your golden rays of divine healing.

Protection Prayer
I pray to the cosmic mother
she who is all things
and ask for ultimate protection
keep me safe
embrace me in your warmth and light.

FOUR

The Altar

A Wiccan's altar is a physical space set aside for meaningful worship, rituals, blessings, and sacred magick. Respected as a place of comfort and power, the altar is as unique as each practitioner and is often personalized with great detail.

The altar is to Wiccans what a church is for Christians. It is a place where prayers are heard, messages are sent, tears of both sadness and joy spring free. The altar is more than a simple table or small shelf, it is a creation that directly links practitioners to the divine.

Once an altar is found (or created), set up, and blessed, the process isn't nearly complete or finished. When Wiccans encounter new spiritual stages, it reflects outwardly upon their altar. Growth from an awakening or overcoming a challenge might influence the practitioner to add more items of significance. Likewise, confronting the past could inspire the removal of tools no longer needed. Through such transference and shifts of energy this sacred space is an ever-evolving process.

This chapter will take you step by step, explaining how to set up an altar that not only reflects the inner you but your beautiful journey on the Wiccan path.

Your altar should be a true expression from the heart.
—ARIAWN, AGE 19, OHIO, USA

Altar Selection: Part One

Altars come in different shapes and sizes. For young adult practitioners the altar is usually kept in the bedroom. Since we aren't all blessed with roomy personal sanctuaries, space becomes a major factor when considering an altar. A small budget is most likely the second factor. However all of this can be dealt with if incorporated into the process ahead of time. And hey, you never know, your future altar may be right under your nose.

Your altar is a sacred space that focuses on the magickal, mundane, and everything in between. It is your sacred space in which you are truly free to experience the Divinity in whatever form you connect with.
—ANUBIS RAINHAWK, AGE 15, CALIFORNIA, USA

Walk into your room and look around. Do you see anything that could be transformed into an altar? Top section of a dresser you could clear off, a desk you don't use, or the side table next to your bed? If you came up emptyhanded or feel that your prospects don't match the mental image you already had in mind, there are other ways to find something more suitable.

My own altar has changed multiple times. I started with a vanity table, at one point I used a cloth-covered cardboard box, and later, a wrought-iron plant holder with a clear glass top. Each of those worked at the time but, eventually I wanted something more. I wanted a lasting altar that fit all of my needs and was visually appealing.

To help the process and send my intention into the universe, I envisioned myself sitting at my dream altar. For weeks I searched and waited. It took a bit of time and help from my mom's keen eye, but one day at a local garage sale we found it! My mom spotted the table first. It was made of white wrought iron and a frosted glass top. I was interested; the condition, size, and shape were all perfect, but I didn't like the color. My mom had a novel idea—spray paint! Then, I knew with a little bit of work, it would become the altar I had always hoped for.

*What's on your altar isn't nearly as important as what it repre-
sents.*
—ANUBIS RAINHAWK, AGE 15, CALIFORNIA, USA

*I have an altar that is actually a wooden microwave cart, al-
though my brother had used it as a bedside stand for a long time.
It is funny because my brother offered it to me at the exact same
time I decided I wanted to keep an altar. So I took it, painted it
with vines, flowers, and some rub-on animal decals, and began
placing my tools on it.*
—ARIAWN, AGE 19, OHIO, USA

Altar Selection: Part Two

Although wood is often suggested by traditional Wiccans because it is derived from nature, your altar can be made of any
substance. Consider the following items and their potential
to be transformed from hopelessly normal to beautifully bewitching:

- Flat Top Trunk or Chest
- Coffee Table
- Wall Shelf (not recommended for burning candles)
- Breakfast-in-Bed Serving Tray
- Sturdy Hatbox
- Decorative Step Stool

Creativity and a bit of hard work can go a long way, but
you'll still need a plan! When searching for your altar, it is a
great idea to decide ahead of time what specific attributes you

are seeking. Express your answers to the following questions in your Book of Shadows.

Which shapes interest you the most?

Round represents cycles, a common theme found throughout the Wiccan path. Square or rectangle shapes symbolize balance and the four elements.

What height would you like your altar to be?

Mine is close to the ground, allowing me to sit and get comfortable without having to reach up high.

What colors do you have in mind? Are you seeking a style and material that will fit in with your room?

❧ From Gwinevere's Book of Shadows

December 21, 2000—Age 16

As I write this I am still shaking. It was toward the end of my Yule ritual and I had a charcoal block and loose incense burning in a glass ashtray. I started to stand up and read a final passage of my ritual when I heard a *crack!* I saw that it was the ashtray, broken straight in half. I was shocked as I saw the orange embers glowing and felt the emanating heat.

I called my mom, who was out in the living room. Since she knew I was doing a ritual, she asked if she should bring water. I replied, "Yes." She came in and poured water over the embers; they sizzled, smoked, and finally went out. In the end with quick thinking, it turned out all right, but I don't think I'll use charcoal incense for a long while!

If you're looking at something used, like a table, remember to check stability. Will it wobble? Are the legs loose? How much time and effort are you willing to put into refurbishing? Are you able to enlist an adult's help if you intend to spray paint?

And finally, what is your budget? How much money can you spend?

> As a teen Wiccan, I have learned that you can pretty much use anything for your altar. I use my dresser.
> —ANUBIS RAINHAWK, AGE 15, CALIFORNIA, USA

❧ From Gwinevere's Book of Shadows

June 16, 2001—Age 16

As I was reading one of my Wicca books, I had experienced something that can only be explained as a vision. I saw in my mind an image of an altar setup so I quickly grabbed a piece of paper and inscribed the basic placements. I have this feeling it is supposed to help me decorate and arrange my next altar.

Setting Up

After you have found a sturdy altar to work with and fixed it to your liking, the next step is finding a place to put it! Generally, Wiccans face the altar toward the north because it is associated with earth, a central element in Wicca. It is believed to be the direction where power flows. Other traditions place the altar in the east, in honor of the rising sun and moon. Feng Shui is a fun alternative to locating the perfect space for your new altar.

*My altar is a small, wooden rectangular table, which I keep in the
back of my room. This piece of work represents my ancestral her-
itage and the roots of my power.*
—PYTHO, AGE 14, MILAN, ITALY

ALTAR CLOTHS

Covering the top of your altar with a special cloth is optional. It
really depends on the type of altar you have and how much of it
you want to see. Maybe, it needs a little color or sprucing up and
a beautiful cloth would do the trick. If your altar is a work of art
already, there is no need to cover something so nice. As an important side note, cloths can be a fire hazard. In this regard, glass
tops are optimal because if a candle accidentally tips over it would
probably blow out; cloths don't have that advantage. Not to mention you can peel candle wax off glass once it dries. In my experience it's more difficult to pry candle wax off fabric. At any rate,
the choice is up to you, but please take into account both the visual benefits of an altar cloth and safety issues associated with it.
Try to decide both what works best for you and your practice.

❧ From Gwinevere's Book of Shadows

August 10, 1999—Age 15

I made my own altar cloth. Over the course of several days I embroidered witchy symbols on the soft, cream-colored fabric. The only issue
is that it's too long for my altar. I have to sort of fold here and there to
make it fit and see my embroidered art. There is something comforting about making my own altar cloth. I know it's filled with my personal power and love.

ALTAR BLESSING RITUAL

Before you proceed to lay out any tools or special items, I highly suggest performing a ritual to cleanse and empower your new altar. What follows is a two-part rite designed to first banish any negativity from the altar and then infuse it with positive and personal vibrations.

Part One

Supplies

A black gemstone such as onyx or obsidian (as an alternative, find a dark-colored rock from outside)

One teaspoon salt

Bowl of water

To begin, request the presence of the Goddess and God by speaking a small invocation. Pick up the black stone and hold it in your palm, close your eyes, and take several deep breaths, softly inhaling and exhaling.

Next, visualize a white light surrounding your hand. Charge the stone with your energy and intention. Once you've finished your visualization, open your eyes and say:

> *"Blessed now is this moment in time*
> *as I caste my spell with enchanted rhyme."*

Place the stone in the center of your altar. Remove your hands from the area and speak this incantation out loud:

> *"Stone of earth, black as night*
> *banish negativity from this site,*
> *under moon, soft and still*
> *this is my wish and earnest will."*

Leave your stone on the altar for at least five minutes. If possible, visualize negativity (as a dark mist) coming from your altar moving into the stone. While the stone is filtering the negative energy, mix the salt and water together. Stir in a clockwise fashion.

After you feel the stone has absorbed all of the lingering negativity, quickly pick it up and drop it into the bowl of salt water. Leave it submerged in the bowl overnight. The saltwater mixture will dissipate and clear any negative energy that the stone had absorbed during the ritual.

Part Two
   Supplies
   Ritual broom
   One stick of either frankincense, myrrh, or sandalwood incense
   Incense holder

Gather your supplies and bring them to your altar. Take the broom and hold it close to the bottom. Position it over your altar toward the northernmost part. Move the broom slowly in a clockwise motion around the altar while saying this chant three times:

   "Bristle of broom
   stalk and staff
   I craft thy magick
   swift and fast."

Put your broom aside and proceed to light the incense stick. Slowly, move the incense over the altar in the same clockwise motion as the broom while saying:

"O'billowing smoke, stirred circle round
protect my sacred space from sky to ground."

When you've completed a full circle, smudge out the stick or place it in an incense holder. Next, using visualization and your index finger trace the following Goddess and God symbols in the center of your altar:

Goddess Symbol

God Symbol

Conclude the ritual by speaking the following blessing:

"May the powers of the Lord and Lady bless this altar space
By the sacred symbols I now trace
As I will so mote it be."

DEITY REPRESENTATIONS
One of the core purposes of having an altar is to show respect and reverence for the Goddess and God. Over time, this sacred space is used to help foster a connection between the practitioner and higher powers. By placing representations of the Lord and Lady on the altar it symbolizes their essence, ultimately making it easier to establish a connection.

Consider the following ideas for your deity representations:

- Use colored candles. Goddess colors are green, blue, or silver. For the God, orange, gold, red, or yellow colors work well.

- Alternatively, white candles can be used for both the Goddess and God. The simplicity of this color is equally meaningful yet understated.

- Statues or sculptures of specific deities, such as Diana or generalized by type, such as Earth Goddess or Solar God.

- An image of Goddess art or nature. For easy display, place photo/image in a small frame. Hang on the wall above altar if you need extra altar space.

- Tap into your artistic side by creating your own deity-inspired drawing, painting, or collage.

- Utilize lunar and solar items such as charms, seasonal decorations, or celestial art.

For the layout I separated the God and Goddess statues and candles to keep toward the back—Goddess on the left and God on the right with the Spirit candle in the middle, and the rest of it is organized by the elements in their respective compass placements.
—ARIAWN, AGE 19, OHIO, USA

After you have decided upon and found representations for the Goddess and God, you'll want to place them on your altar. As a rule of thumb, the Goddess energy is concentrated on the left and the God energy is on the right. If you disagree with this concept, follow your intuition and figure out what works for you.

It is also important to realize that deity representations will change and evolve over time. You aren't stuck with the same items you started out with. It can take a while to find something "just right" but don't presume that a temporary representation would hurt your practice. The higher powers aren't picky about how you honor them. They care about your experience, interaction, prayers, rituals, and spiritual quest.

❧ From Gwinevere's Book of Shadows
November 25, 2002—Age 18
For years now I've shopped around seeking deity statues. The ones that I've come across don't call to me. Until the day comes when I have my "A-ha, I've found it!" moment, I'll continue to use taper candles to represent the energy of the Goddess and God. These tall cream candles have become a symbol for me, and each time I see them I know someday soon the right statues will come along.

My altar design changes as I change. I decorate it in certain ways during the Sabbats, Esbats, and special rituals. Depending on the season I might have flowers, leaves, or stones to decorate my altar.
—ANUBIS RAINHAWK, AGE 15, CALIFORNIA, USA

ELEMENT REPRESENTATIONS
The elements: earth, air, fire, and water are the essentials of nature and hold a vast reservoir of energy. Wiccans seek to tap into this emanating power for use in both magick and ritual. Certain attributes are linked to each element. Below you'll find this info and suggestions on how to represent all four on your altar.

Earth is a feminine element, linked to the direction of north. Spiritual qualities of earth are: stabilizing, fertile, nourishing, nurturing, growth, and abundance. Magickal associations include: money, prosperity, employment, luck, healing, fertility, and beauty.

Representations: Jar or bowl of either salt, sand, dirt, or herb mixture. Additionally, a green candle could be used to symbolize the element of earth.

Air is a masculine element, linked to the direction of east. Spiritual qualities of air are: movement, inspiration, communication, intellect, and awareness. Magickal associations include: wisdom, creativity, new beginnings, and psychic awareness.

Representations: Feather, incense, or silver bell. Additionally, a white or yellow candle could be used to symbolize the element of air.

Fire is a masculine element, linked to the direction of south. Spiritual qualities of fire are: transformation, change, strength, courage, passion, sexuality, and sensuality. Magickal associations include: protection, warding, increasing energy, building power, desire, and success.

Representations: Reddish-orange crystal/gemstone such as citrine, carnelian, or tiger's eye. Additionally, a red candle could be used to symbolize the element of fire.

Water is a feminine element, linked to the direction of the west. Spiritual qualities of water are tranquillity, intuition, emotion, psychic energy, subconscious, cleansing, and blessing. Magickal associations include: sleep, prophetic dreams, meditation, peace, purification, healing, love, and friendship.

Representations: Seashell, piece of smoothed white or green glass from the ocean, jar or bowl of either tapwater, rainwater, or Full Moon–blessed water. (See chapter Eight for more details on creating Full Moon–blessed water.) Additionally, a blue candle could be used to symbolize the element of water.

Generally I divide my altar into four sections, which correspond to the four elements and their associated directions. At east I place a stick of incense; at north I place a rock or pentagram ring; at west I place a chalice of moon water; and at South a tea-light candle. On top of this generic layout I place one candle on the right-hand side to represent the God, and one on the left-hand side to represent the Goddess.

—GEDE, AGE 15, QUEENSLAND, AUSTRALIA

In regard to altar placement, you have the option of assigning each element representation a specific space. You might even choose to link the element with its associated direction (this information is indicated in the correspondences above). However, I have found that directional placement for the element representations isn't necessary. So long as each element is displayed on your altar in some way, shape, or form, the energy will be present, creating both harmony and balance.

RITUAL TOOLS

While a Wiccan weaves a ritual in both heart and mind, the practitioner calls upon specific tools to set the mood and link the spiritual and physical worlds. If one needs to banish negativity, caste a circle, or empower an object, there is a tool to lend its support.

In addition to tapping into our sense through the sight of dancing candle flames, methodical movements of a sweeping broom, and the scent of smouldering incense we also spark and awaken our ritual consciousness through their consistent use.

The tools can either be crafted, store-bought, second-hand discoveries, or a comfortable mixture of all three. Try not to feel overwhelmed if you are first starting your collection. There is adventure in gradually finding new items to add. In regard to tool placement, some suggest laying them out according to the elements or masculine/feminine associations. In my experience, a keen eye combined with intuition works just as well!

Below is a list of the tools that are most often used by Wiccans. When reading the descriptions, carefully weigh out which ones would benefit your practice, as you probably won't need all of them. Remember, what might be essential to one person may not be to another.

When I'm starting the ritual, I place my tools carefully on the altar and they seem to find their right place. The layout also depends on what I'm going to do. If I need to read, I have to put the Book of Shadows on the altar in a way that it can be opened.
—LUNA, AGE 16, FINLAND

My tools are positioned in the places that they "tell me" to be placed. I'll touch the item, then have it draw my hand to the place that feels appropriate.
—PYTHO, AGE 14, MILAN, ITALY

Broom

The ritual broom, sometimes called a *besom*, has both masculine and feminine associations. Its main function is to rid an area, circle, or sacred space of negativity. To do this the practitioner walks around the circle one to three times in a clockwise manner with broom in hand, bristles barely touching the floor as if sweeping the air. Combined with visualization, this action chases away any negative energy or psychic residue in the area. Additionally, some Wiccan couples jump over the broom during handfastings (weddings) to encourage a fertile and successful union. Brooms come in a wide variety of styles and lengths. It can be elaborately decorated or kept in its natural state. Due to its connection with cleansing it is linked with the element of water.

Wand

The magick wand is associated with the God and masculine energy. As a primary tool, it has multiple functions in ritual. Wiccans use a wand to cast the sacred circle, call the corners, and invoke the higher powers. The magick wand is a conduit, moving and focusing your energy to empower an object or space. Although most often made of wood (from a fallen branch) this tool can also be created from other substances such as a terminated quartz crystal, glass tube, or thin copper pipe. If you have an interest in making your own wand, research the different types of wood available to you and perhaps consider alternative materials for something more unique. The magick wand is linked to the direction of east and element of air.

Athame

The Athame is a double-edged ritual knife associated with the God and masculine energy. It is used to cast the sacred circle, call the corners, direct energy, consecrate, and channel personal power. Athames are not meant to cut physical objects, only energy—therefore, it is customary for the blade to remain dull. Sizes vary; I have seen some as small as four and a half inches to ones reaching beyond a foot. Traditionally the athame has a black handle, which aids in drawing power. It can be left plain or personalized by either engraving symbols on the handle or adorning it with ribbons, charms, and crystals. As an instrument of change and manipulation the athame is linked to the element of fire. Compare the athame with the wand, as both tools play similar roles in rituals. To conserve both space and money, decide which one suits you the most.

Altar Pentacle

The altar pentacle, which incorporates the main symbol associated with Wicca, has both masculine and feminine properties. This ritual tool is flat, usually disk-shaped and inscribed with a five-pointed star encased in a circle. It is utilized for purposes of protection, blessing, and consecration. For this reason, some practitioners place bowls of water or salt on top of the pentacle. Likewise, charms, cords, and other spell ingredients can be kept there to purify, empower, and protect. During special rituals, mini cakes, cookies, and crackers might be placed on there for a special Goddess blessing. To form this sacred tool, the pentacle symbol can either be painted, engraved, or inlaid on a wide variety of materials such as a smoothed stone, piece of slate, ceramic title, colored glass, molded clay, craved wood, pewter, copper, or brass. When crafting or purchasing one, make sure that it is visually appealing and in proportion with your altar space. Due to its ability to repel negativity as well as ground and protect, the altar pentacle is linked to the element of earth.

Chalice

The chalice or ritual cup is associated with the Goddess and feminine energy. It is a special goblet set aside from everyday glassware and only used for ritual purposes. The chalice might be ornate in design with engraved symbols and etchings, or plain and understated. This ritual item can be made of pewter (specifically look for lead-free pewter), silver, brass, crystal or if necessary, plastic. Practitioners usually fill the chalice with a drink associated with a particular holiday or event. Apple juice (or cider) creates a festive mood for fall; eggnog for winter; punch for spring; and orange juice for hot summer months. The contents are usually consecrated or blessed for the occasion. Due to its use for liquid, the chalice is linked to the element of water.

Cauldron

The cauldron is associated with the Goddess and feminine energy. Contrary to popular myth, this tool isn't used for boiling potions. Practitioners of Wicca creatively incorporate this item into their Sabbat celebrations by filling it with seasonal decorations: dried corn husks for fall; evergreens for winter; wildflowers for spring; candles floating in water for summer. Additionally, sturdy fireproof cauldrons have been incorporated into spell work. For example, if change is desired, a wish paper is lit on fire and dropped into the cauldron to burn, initiating the transformation process. I have two cauldrons: one is small, about three inches in diameter and made of cast iron (a thick metal) with three legs, symbolic of the triple Goddess. The other is an old copper simmering pot that is larger in size, about five inches in diameter with no legs yet still has a cupped belly shape. This ritual tool has deep symbolism representing wisdom, inspiration, and regeneration. It is aligned with the element of water.

> ### ❧ From Gwinevere's Book of Shadows
> *February 28, 2000—Age 15*
> While trying to give a boost to my memory for an upcoming French quiz, the other day I created a spell that incorporated burning a piece of paper and throwing it into my cauldron. It ended up burning safely but filling my whole room with smoke. I had to open the windows to get it out and went to sleep with a yucky burnt smell in my room.

Incense Burner

The incense burner, sometimes referred to as a censer, is associated with the element of air. Used to burn ignited incense, this tool's appearance varies upon the form of incense used. What follows is a description of the three types of incense and their holders. Self-igniting charcoal disks, which are found specially at new age/metaphysical stores (supposedly beneficial due to their abilities to burn personally blended incense mixtures of dried herbs, flowers, resins, and spices), can be the hardest to light and often present safety issues. If you do intend on using this kind of incense it is important to find a heat-resistant container and fill the bottom with an inch of salt or sand before putting the lit charcoal in. Joss incense (thin, ten-inch sticks) are the easiest to find and use. Light the tip, wait a moment, and then blow out the flame to expose a glowing ember, which releases a heavenly scent. Stick incense burners are about ten-and-a-half inches long, one-and-a-half inches in width, and fairly flat. They can be made of ceramic, soapstone, pewter, or wood.

Joss incense is my favorite and what I recommend most to other practitioners for ritual use. Cone incense (about three centimeters in height) may not be as widely available as the joss sticks or come in as many scents, but it is the incense to use if space is limited on your altar. Cone incense burners range from the ornate three-legged brass censer, to the creative seashell filled with sand, to the super-spacesaver ceramic disk. No matter which type you choose to work with, it is important that you realize incense is more than something to smell. Playing a subtle yet important role, it is used to purify sacred space, enhance your atmosphere, and bring out your magical mind-set. Overall, incense is a wonderfully diverse tool for your altar.

Aside from the tools already mentioned, there are several other items that can be found on a Wiccan's altar.

- A bowl or jar of **salt** is kept on hand to consecrate items; likewise, **Full Moon–blessed** water provides similar blessing properties.

- Extra **candles** (in proper holders) help illuminate the area. I keep two taper candles toward the back of my altar, which add additional light for a nighttime spell or ritual.

- An **oil burner** is an alternative option for those who dislike incense.

- A **candle snuffer** may be an important tool to add to your collection if you cringe at the notion of blowing out your candles.

- Place your **divination tools** (e.g., tarot, runes, pendulum) in a drawstring pouch on your altar for safekeeping and easy access.

- Lastly, store a **lighter** (for candles) along with other knick-knacks in an **altar box or basket**.

On my altar, I have gathered dried roses, seashells, and salt in a beautiful jar.
—LUNA, AGE 16, FINLAND

❧ From Gwinevere's Book of Shadows

October 2, 2001—Age 17

I used to think that my altar had to have no more and no less than what tools the beginner books suggested. Then I woke up and realized, this is my special place! I should be able to create it however I see fit. Once things came into focus, I slowly started to add small trinkets and mementoes. The feeling of my altar changed. I added a wrought-iron metal basket to hold these special objects along with basic altar necessities like a lighter, salt in a bottle, and my candle snuffer.

ALTAR DEVOTIONS

An altar devotion is a daily or weekly practice that helps the practitioner develop a special rapport with divinity. It is a time out from life problems, family issues, and school stress. The process isn't complicated; you simply sit before the altar, calm yourself through deep breaths, and consciously link your spirit to the higher powers.

You can take the opportunity to pray, meditate, talk out fears, read poetry, or write in your Book of Shadows. By consistently repeating this informal ritual you will not only attune yourself with the higher powers but reap mental and emotional benefits as well. In my experience this basic act of honoring deity has opened my soul, given a boost to my self-esteem, and improved positive thinking.

Although I wish I had the chance to partake in an altar devotion every day, I make sure to find the time once a week. Remember, these few minutes are for awareness and to give thanks, not for casting spells.

You'll most benefit from the experience if you can set aside a prescribed day (perhaps every Saturday) or time (such as after breakfast). This rhythmic consistency builds a spiritual foundation and helps you align your energy with the higher powers.

Below is my format for an altar devotion. Since this is such a personal ritual, feel free to change it to suit your own needs.

Altar Devotion Ritual
   Supplies
   Your altar
   Stick of incense
   At least ten minutes of privacy

Set the mood by lighting candles for illumination and igniting incense. Get comfortable before your altar and look to your deity representations. Take a deep breath and exhale slowly while visualizing a white mist coming into your body and calming you down. Repeat these deep breaths two more times with continued visualization. When you're ready, recite this prayer:

> *"I call to the Great Divine*
> *Warm solar burst of loving vibrations*
> *In the noon day sky*
> *Earthen mother source of creation*
> *Enchanting all phases and time*
> *My heart is open*
> *For your love to roam wild and free*
> *As I give thanks for my life, a beautiful blessing."*

For a few moments, reflect on the prayer's meaning: opening your heart to deity and giving thanks. Utilize the rest of your time in any way you wish—meditate, express thoughts or concerns, read poetry, write in your Book of Shadows, or make preparations for an upcoming Sabbat.

Once you feel that your altar devotion is winding down, look to your deity representations and softly speak this closing statement:

"My Goddess and God
This ritual has come to an end
Until next time
Merry part and blessed be!"

Extinguish any lit candles, incense, and tidy up your altar space. Proceed with your day.

FIVE

Life and Wicca

've always thought that being a teenager is a full-time job. Add Wicca into the mix and who knows what can happen! One of the reasons I created this chapter is to tackle the subject of being a Wiccan in today's society. Here you'll find information on coming out of the broom closet and how image and stereotypes factor into this path. In addition there is a section for male practitioners, which includes a ritual to connect with one's inner God, and dragon invocations.

Coming Out of the Broom Closet

For many practitioners Wicca is slowly integrated into one's life over the course of time. The term *converting* seems awkward, as if it is quick and happens in a single moment. In my personal experience the process of leaving my old path and coming to

Wicca was softer and more subtle. I barely noticed the transition because it felt so natural. After this change critical questions arose. I began to wonder, Should I tell someone about the choice I've made? Who can I discuss this with and will they understand? It's a challenge that each Wiccan faces—coming out to voice their newfound faith.

It's important to realize that since Wicca isn't widely known, family members may not have even heard of the term until you've mentioned it to them. Part of your responsibility is then defining the Wiccan path along with its practices. Over the next few pages I'll show you how and when to convey your faith to the ones you love. Before we proceed, it is vital you know what choices you have in regard to this matter. You have the option of expressing your beliefs relatively soon, at some point down the line, or delaying and withholding the information indefinitely. It is my sincere hope that after reviewing this section you'll make an informed decision on which course of action is right for you and your life.

Closet is a term that is sometimes used metaphorically to denote a hidden part of one's life. When politicians have skeletons in the closet, it means they have a lurid secret. It is also applied to hiding sexual preference. "In" is a shortened slang version for being in the closet. "Out" refers to being out of the closet. Wiccans add broom to the beginning of the term to distinguish our notion of withholding the identity of our religion, from the other types mentioned above. Even though the words *broom closet* sound cute, this is a serious subject that eventually affects each practitioner.

Avoiding the issue of whether or not to come out of the broom closet will only compound your anxiety. If you address the situation head-on and get to the root of your fears, your choices will unfold. Empower yourself by looking at the whole picture and assessing each of your options.

The best advice I can give is to come out slowly. Give people a chance to know who you are before letting them know what you are.
—Chiron Nightwolf, age 16, Georgia, USA

CIRCUMSTANCES AND ENVIRONMENT

Although Wiccans are united by faith, each of our lives and circumstances vary. Some practitioners have liberal, open-minded family and friends, while others are surrounded by more conservative and devoutly religious loved ones. Aside from political or religious beliefs, our human nature evokes the desire to be accepted by the people close to us. This can lead to anxious feelings about expressing one's new path. Concerns over being misunderstood, rejected, or ostracized are well-founded and completely understandable.

The key to preventing misunderstandings is to find the right words beforehand to define your path. Misinterpretations can also be fixed by a follow-up e-mail or quick phone call. Fear of rejection is natural. If you are pushed away by a friend because you are Wiccan, it goes to show they probably aren't worthy of your companionship. Don't you want to surround yourself with people who care about you and accept all of your faults, differences, and quirks? The very definition of a friend is based on trust, counting on one another, and believing in each other through the good times and the bad.

Sometimes people mock or ridicule things that they don't understand. Being ostracized, put down, or made fun of are never good feelings and can be especially challenging to deal with in school. I had a few peers joke around with me about being Wiccan. One guy asked me to prove my "magick powers" by turning him into a frog. Although that case was well-natured, there can be more hurtful things said in the guise of teasing.

The best way to combat this type of behavior is to make an example of yourself. If you take Wicca seriously, others will be more inclined to as well.

Environment also plays a significant role in whether or not young adults feel comfortable in coming out. In real estate there is a popular saying: Location, location, location. Roughly speaking, it means the appeal and practicality of a particular area. What does this have to do with Wicca? Everything! Well-known and even joked about are the social, cultural, and lifestyle differences between the northern and southern parts of the United States.

Born and raised in New York and having moved to Florida a few years ago, I came to realize an underlying variation between what I was accustomed to and southern ways. For example, burgers offered with mustard, normal to Florida eateries, are mostly unheard of in New York. The south often touts expressions like southern "charm" or "hospitality," which conjure up images of people eating peach cobbler or sipping iced tea on front porches. Likewise, a strong belief in church spread across several states earns parts of the south the infamous label of the Bible Belt. This concept brings comfort to Christians, Baptists, and Evangelicals. However, for non-Christians, it can create a struggle to embrace and practice one's own belief system.

Even though aspects of the south are slowly changing and evolving, living here means taking into consideration the Bible Belt and presence of the Christian church not only in private homes, but in the hearts and minds of southern society.

YOUR OPTIONS
Certain variables have an impact on whether teen Wiccans decide to come out or stay in the broom closet. The following is a list of points that highlight these relevant issues.

Pros of Coming Out

Opportunity of religious expression such as wearing a pentacle in public.

Being able to read books on Wicca without hiding them.

Having the option of displaying an altar to honor the higher powers and work magick.

Ability to find and converse with other Wiccans in the area.

Being able to educate others by dispelling Wiccan stereotypes.

Not having to lie or keep secrets.

Pros of Staying In

Keeping yourself emotionally and physically safe.

Not having to worry about being rejected by family or friends.

Using the time to learn more about the path before considering coming out.

Maintaining job security—for example, if you baby-sit for a devoutly religious family and revealing your beliefs would cause a negative reaction.

Continue to receive regular treatment at school by teachers and peers.

Avoiding awkward moments or fights with family.

Now that you have carefully reviewed each of the points, try to consider how these situations might occur in your life. Which group identifies most with your priorities? How does the comparison of expression versus security factor in your mind? Jot down your thoughts, emotions, or concerns on this subject in your Book of Shadows.

> 🌿 From Gwinevere's Book of Shadows
>
> *January 10, 2004—Age 19*
>
> I worry that teen practitioners feel pressured by the Wiccan community to "come out of the broom closet." I wish that the world was more accepting of us, but that will take more time. We already have so much to be concerned about, so until that safe point I feel like young people shouldn't have this extra pressure. I realize how lucky I am. My family has made an effort to understand my path, but others don't have that support. Maybe Wiccans who are out of the closet could be more compassionate. Just because staying in may not be the popular choice doesn't mean it shouldn't be discussed as an option. This attacking one another over personal decisions upsets me. I want it to come to an end.

No one else can ever tell you what is right or wrong for you. That is something you need to decide for yourself. With that in mind, ensure that you are very much aware of your decision to consciously come out of the broom closet.
—GEDE, AGE 15, QUEENSLAND, AUSTRALIA

Since you're mulling over the idea of coming out, I have another note of interest. Young Wiccans who are out usually find a certain level at which they are comfortable expressing their beliefs. Some find it easy to tell one parent and a couple friends. Others are more willing to put themselves out there and tell everyone. I've even known teens to do research papers on this contemporary religion—talk about openness and expression!

Do you know what degree you would like to be open as a Wiccan? Do you have a mental list of people you're considering telling? To help you figure out this situation, I've created a quick quiz. It will also show you how well you know the people in your life. Give some thought to the question concerning each person before you circle your answer.

If I told my best friend *I was Wiccan the next time I saw him/her, he/she would . . .*
a) freak out b) need time to get used to my choice c) be accepting of my beliefs d) don't know

If I told my mother *I was Wiccan the next time I saw her, she would . . .*
a) freak out b) need time to get used to my choice c) be accepting of my beliefs d) don't know

If I told my father *I was Wiccan the next time I saw him, he would . . .*
a) freak out b) need time to get used to my choice c) be accepting of my beliefs d) don't know

If I told my close friends *I was Wiccan the next time I saw them, they would . . .*
a) freak out b) need time to get used to my choice c) be accepting of my beliefs d) don't know

If I told my siblings *I was Wiccan the next time I saw them, they would . . .*
a) freak out b) need time to get used to my choice c) be accepting of my beliefs d) don't know

If I told my grandparents *I was Wiccan the next time I saw them, they would . . .*
a) freak out b) need time to get used to my choice c) be accepting of my beliefs d) don't know

Now that you have considered specific people and their possible reactions, how does it reflect your initial choice of staying in or coming out? What impact has this made on your decision? If you chose "a" for the majority of your answers, don't be discouraged. This isn't the end of the road. Sometimes you might anticipate a negative reaction only to receive a positive one in return.

It can be difficult to determine how someone will feel about your Wiccan path until you actually express your beliefs to them. This is why being prepared and well informed is essential to coming out. You can't control someone else's reaction, but you can control how, when, and why you come out.

This next section is one of the most important parts of the whole book. Even if you decide you'd like to keep your beliefs a secret, please read this because it holds important tips and suggestions on dealing with all aspects of this subject.

WAYS AND METHODS

Coming out is a one-shot deal that you cannot take back, so be sure that voicing your path is a step you really want to take. There are good reasons to come out, but also ones that can come back to haunt you. For example, using the path as an intimidation tactic or rebellious act of defiance screams of childish behavior and will be completely obvious to the people around you. Likewise, acting in such a way that uses a beautiful path to do harm or wreak havoc not only disrespects yourself, but also the religion. I do know that a large percentage of teen Wiccans are honest and respectful, so let's prove it. If you choose to come out, do so for the right reasons.

Determine why you are going to come out in the first place. What are your intentions? If you're in it for the "image" or to scare people, then chances are you will only be doing more harm than good for a community that is struggling to gain acceptance.
—ARIAWN, AGE 19, OHIO, USA

Additionally, it has to be said if you feel pressured by another person or have a weird sense of obligation to reveal your beliefs, you will come off as insincere. We have free will, the ability to make our own choices, and to do what is best for ourselves. Take advantage of this, listen to your intuition, and follow your heart!

Preparing to come out is equally as instrumental as the actual act. In effect, you're creating a plan of action. The first part of your plan is research. Know what you'll be talking about by getting the facts. How did Wicca originate? What do Wiccans believe in? Since you'll want to be well spoken and knowledgeable on this important discussion topic, get the facts first. With the research prepared in advance you'll appear more confident and be able to answer questions easier.

Always remember to remain calm and mature when you are making the announcement and fielding questions and concerns. Adults and friends will be more willing to accept your choices if you appear to have properly educated yourself, obtained some degree of wisdom, and that your decision was reached with a rational mind. Feel out a situation, search within yourself for your own intent and ability to handle potential repercussions, and keep a level head, and you should be relatively fine.
—ARIAWN, AGE 19, OHIO, USA

Preparation Exercise
Try to anticipate the questions your family and friends might ask and write them down on the front of index cards. In your own words, inscribe the answers on the back. If you come across a difficult question or something you're unsure about, thumb through a few Wicca books or search the Internet. Utilize your cards as if you were studying for an upcoming test.

The next step is carefully considering who you'd like to express your beliefs to first. A trusted friend is often a great place to start, mainly because they know you well, and will probably be around the same age. Often we can tell our friends something with ease that might be more challenging to tell a parent. Use this connection to create a more comfortable start when coming out.

When you feel ready, pick a good setting, preferably a place with privacy and at a time when your mind and your friend's will be clear. For example, a fun weekend day hanging out at the park is a much better setting than sharing this news at school, rushing between classes. Be honest and upfront. Tell them that you want to get something off your chest and hope that you can trust them to be open-minded. Here are a few talking points:

Lately, I've been learning about a religion called Wicca . . .

I think Wicca is the path for me because . . .

There are some crazy stereotypes out there but, Wicca is really about . . .

I know you may be confused so I am open to any questions . . .

Try to avoid overwhelming them with extensive details. You can always fill them in later at a more gradual pace. Because Wiccans don't proselytize (seek to convert people) let your friend know that this is your choice, for yourself and it isn't your intention to get him or her to join your new religion.

After you have taken this brave step and told your trusted friend, take a day to reflect upon the experience before jumping to tell others. Give yourself time to digest the encounter. Learn from your friend's queries and how you handled your responses.

*The best way to make them understand is to show that you're
mature enough to discuss this like an adult and show through
your actions that you're not rebelling against them but finding
your own way to believe.*
—LUNA, AGE 16, FINLAND

There are alternative methods of coming out that don't involve face-to-face communication. A phone call offers warmth without feeling too distant or removed. E-mail on the other hand, probably won't bear the best results, especially because there is a lack of interaction and may create a challenge in maintaining a personal or comforting tone.

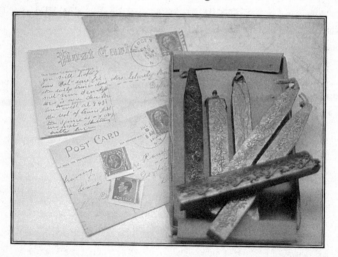

In her book *The Real Witches' Handbook,* author Kate West suggests a handwritten letter, as does teen contributor Anubis Rain-Hawk. He spoke of his own experience, "Eventually, I gained enough courage to tell my parents. . . . I wrote them a letter basically describing Wicca, my beliefs, and why I believe them. Along with the note, I left a few books so that they could read about my beliefs, and hopefully, understand and respect them."

While this may work for some, especially the shy or nervous Wiccan, letters (and e-mails) may be shared with more than the one person you initially anticipated it for. Putting your path in writing might have the same impact as offering your personal thoughts to any one who gets their hands on it.

Even with careful preparation and deciding upon your method of expression coming out to "the parents" is one of the most challenging tasks for a young Wiccan. When I told my mother about my interest in Wicca, I received an inquisitive but positive reaction. However, I do understand that coming out to one's parents can be a daunting task, as I speak with many teens over the Internet and have heard a wide range of reactions from parents, both the good and bad. The one consistent theme among those teens whose parents were more tolerant and respectful is the teen's conduct during the discussion. Fighting or raising your voice will only bring more chaos to the situation. Try your best to remain calm, cool, and collected. This way you'll set the mood and show that the discussion can remain cordial.

> *Telling my parents about my spirituality was extremely difficult. It hurt that I couldn't speak of my spiritual beliefs with them, because it's something special and sacred to me. Eventually, I gained enough courage to tell my parents. When my parents found out I was Wiccan, they weren't exactly thrilled. We had long and painful talks for months. Fortunately, they eventually understood that I had different beliefs. Now I study and practice freely.*
> —Anubis RainHawk, age 15, California, USA

> *At first, I had no idea how to tell my mom about my interest in Wicca. Eventually, I sat her down and expressed that Wicca was something I could see myself living by the rest of my life. I*

explained that I was much happier as a Wiccan than I had ever been has a Christian. She was kind of freaked out and had some questions, which I answered as best I could. In the end my mom was okay with me practicing Wicca. It was a big relief.
—LYNX SONG, AGE 15, LOUISIANA, USA

AFTER YOU COME OUT

After you come out to family and friends, things might feel tense or uncomfortable. Constant communication and time are the best ways to overcome those awkward moments. Give your loved ones several opportunities to ask questions and voice their concerns. Show them that you are still the same amazing person that they have always known and hopefully you can start to enjoy living a more public Wiccan life.

Unfortunately, not all parents will understand your spiritual path. Even if they disapprove, you will always have magick within you. Wicca is not about spells or rituals; it is about your spiritual journey.
—ANUBIS RAINHAWK, AGE 15, CALIFORNIA, USA

There are message boards for teen Wiccans all over the Net. Such online communities can be a valuable source of support. Perform a quick web search using terms like *teen Wicca chat* or *teen Wicca group*. It is a comforting feeling once you realize that you aren't alone and there are others going through the same thing.

Once you are "out," it's important to realize that some Wiccans aren't able or ready to do the same. If a friend is a closeted Wiccan, try your best to support them and their decision anyway. Sometimes, we need to respect others even when we don't agree with their choices. Besides, you can't walk in their shoes or experience every detail of their life.

> 🌿 From Gwinevere's Book of Shadows
>
> *February 2000—Age 15*
>
> In my social studies class a so-called-friend was upset with this obnoxious guy, so she turns to him and says, "Watch out or she'll put a curse on you" while pointing toward me. The teacher changed the subject before I could really say anything. I don't mind that everyone knows about me being Wiccan. I just don't want people to believe in the stereotype of practitioners cursing other people. I really should have a talk with this girl. I don't want to get in trouble for things I haven't even said or done!

Religion is a sensitive topic. If a parent or friend can't get used to your path, it's okay to agree to disagree and not bring up the subject when they are around. Hopefully with the right preparation and approach, your coming out will be a positive growing experience.

Ethics and Image

In chapter Two we discussed how Wiccan ethics are beneficial for your personal development, spiritual insight, and karmic future, but they also affect your everyday conduct and improve the way you are perceived. This may come as a surprise but, as a Wiccan you could be viewed by your classmates, friends, or family as a representative of the Craft. Many young adult Wiccans are elected into this position without even realizing it.

I am sharing this insight with you not to put on additional pressure, but to open your eyes and level of awareness. People will be watching you, listening to the things you say, and some-times associating those things with your religion. I don't like it but unfortunately its the way the world works. If a group of Wiccans dabble in illegal drugs, then people might assume Wicca is lax about drug use. We know the truth, how "Harm none" includes oneself, but they don't! Whether you like it or not if you're open about your path and "out" as a Wiccan, then your life and how you choose to live it is their example. Con-ducting yourself in a responsible manner is important to the way our religion is viewed. Image is a pivotal step in increasing the awareness and tolerance of this path.

Image vs. Fashion

Often people mistake the concept of image with fashion. A person's image is a mixture of confidence, personality, and a dash of reputation. Fashion is all about clothing, style, and accessories. When you first meet someone the two make a com-bined impact and impression, but often their image remains front and center while fashion seems to gradually fall into the background.

When I mention image as a pivotal step in increasing the awareness and tolerance of this path, I don't mean that all Wic-cans need to walk on eggshells, be perfect in the public eye, or dress a certain way. Be yourself, honor all the beauty that the Goddess has given you! Go places, enjoy your friends, and dress in whatever style you'd like.

This brings up an interesting topic. Several Wiccans have said practitioners who are Goth (prefer to dress in black and have an affinity for darker things) give the religion a bad name. This idea is preposterous. How can a few people's style "bring down" a religion? I understand that piercings, pale skin, dark lipstick, and head-to-toe black outfits aren't for everyone and might make those who don't understand the Goth lifestyle uncomfortable. What I can't wrap my mind around is that it's accepted to use that uncomfortableness as an excuse to degrade anyone who chooses to dress differently. Some people who don't follow the Wiccan religion—and even some who do—are guilty of this prejudice. It's time to stop because in the end, behaving intolerantly toward Gothic Wiccans will give us all a bad image.

I have always been Goth, at least on some level, but to be a Goth and to be Wiccan are different things.
—LUNA, AGE 16, FINLAND

I do not personally consider myself to be Gothic, but I have been called so by others. I dress in black at all times. This is simply because, as with the word night *in my Craft name, the color black resembles the night, and the dark of night symbolizes the universe in whole and the collective energies of all who live in it.*
—CHIRON NIGHTWOLF, AGE 16, GEORGIA, USA

Teen Wiccans Stereotyped

Gothic Wiccans are not the only group being stereotyped. In fact, lots of times teen practitioners get trash-talked by older Wiccans. They think we are just in it for the spells, when the truth is, we love this path for the same reasons they do: It empowers us, opens our minds, and comforts our souls.

To argue the other side, some adults are respectful of young people joining the path. They realize that we are the next generation and one day will be holding high coven positions, tackling politics, and running antidiscrimination organizations. If only more adult practitioners had this view, teen Wiccans could stop feeling as if we aren't accepted in our own religion.

This topic hits me personally. A few years ago, when I was fifteen and living in New York I saw a notice up on a bulletin board in a New Age store. The notice was about a beginners' study group that was forming for local Wiccans. I was excited about the prospect and wanted to meet other practitioners in the area. I eagerly took down the woman's e-mail address and wrote to her the next day.

I informed her that my mother had accepted my path, and asked if I'd be allowed to meet with the study group. Even though the notice hadn't mentioned an age requirement, the woman forming the group wouldn't allow me to join because I didn't fit in with her ideal age criteria.

I was dedicated to my path and knew it was going to stay a part of my life. It was hard for me to understand why I was rejected. Up until that point, I had rarely encountered ageism. For weeks I felt alienated from my own religion.

Eventually, I moved past that pain and over the years came to enjoy solitary work. I supplemented my practice by conversing with other practitioners over the Internet. However, that disappointing experience has always stuck with me and continues in part to fuel my writing and need to connect with other teens.

I'd like to believe that one day in the future, young adults will be more accepted and integrated within our own religion. Until then, if something similar happens to you, don't let anyone pull you down or ruin your Craft. Trust me, you don't want to be involved with snobby "better than thou" Wiccans anyway! Find other teens in your area, create your own magical friendships, and remember solitary work can be equally as wonderful and deeply rewarding.

Actually, my own mentors looked down upon me when I first met them. They ran a chat room on the Internet for a long time, and I had stumbled across it one day. Over time they came to respect me and see that I truly wanted to follow this path.
—Ariawn, age 19, Ohio, USA

No adult Wiccan has ever treated me with any less than equality and respect. Thankfully, I have not come across another practitioner who has seen themselves as superior to me.
—Chiron Nightwolf, age 16, Georgia, USA

When I first started to attend a Pagan social group in my area, I felt that my actions were being constantly judged and dismissed as ignorant and unenlightened. I felt my views and opinions were undermined and disrespected by the older Pagans and that my presence was more of an irritation than anything else. However,

---

🌿 From Gwinevere's Book of Shadows

March 25, 2000—Age 15

My best friend and I walked to a New Age store. It was her first time ever going in one. While we were walking she asked me if the walls would be black and if it's scary. Since I had been in there a long while before I had assured her that things would be okay. When we approached the store it was just as I had remembered, the sound of wind chimes singing in the wind. The interior was pure white walls (not black as my best friend had worried). We both bought incense, the cheapest thing in the store, and hung around talking with the coowner. She was pretty with dark hair and big blue eyes; very witchy. Even though we were young, she treated us with respect and that really meant something to me.

despite my initial anxieties, I continued to attend monthly meet-ings and slowly became accepted into the group.
—GEDE, AGE 15, QUEENSLAND, AUSTRALIA

Negative Catchphrases

Within the past few pages you may have picked up on a common theme: Wiccans putting down other Wiccans. We are always say-ing that other religions don't understand us and aren't tolerant enough, but how can we complain when there is so much in-fighting and name-calling?

Lately, negative catchphrases have been floating around to describe levels of experience and ways of practice. If someone wants to experiment with a few spells but not fully commit to the path they are considered to be a *dabbler*. Testing out the waters, so long as the Rede is taken into consideration shouldn't be viewed as a negative. In fact, it should be seen as an asset, looking into something first, then deciding if it fits. An alternative version of *dabbler* is *wannabe*: an enthusiastic Wiccan new to everything, who overwhelmingly talks about magick-based movies, covens, and cauldrons. Experienced practitioners need to understand that beginners thrive on that "just-starting-out energy." Eventually they'll snap back into real life after they see past the tools, toys, and spells. Having patience with such newcomers is a necessity. Remember, you were once a beginner, too.

Out of all the phrases the one that really gets to me is *fluffy bunny*. It is sometimes used by traditional witches to describe practitioners who only work with positive magick. Those throwing around this negative term argue that Wiccans do not honor the darker aspects of life and nature. However, I believe many Wiccans do acknowledge a darker aspect. We aren't obliv-ious to the notion that different energies exist. Our belief in balance shows us that we need to have darkness in order to have light. Throughout the moon cycle and season, Wiccans are aware of both energies and work with them but in ways that are useful and channeled for positive purposes.

The dark moon (a time that occurs several days leading up to the new moon) can magickally be utilized to hurt or protect. For example if someone is gossiping about you, this moon phase could be used to bring about revenge but an ethical Wiccan would choose to stop the harmful energy and send it into the earth to be neutralized. There is a difference between acknowledging the dark side and seeking it out for destructive purposes. Wiccans look for moral solutions and work to transform nature's energy into positive applications like a healing spell or protection shield.

I don't want to sound preachy but, we need to cut out all the name-calling, labels, and stereotypes. If each person refuses to use the terms *dabbler, wannabe,* and *fluffy bunny* from this point

---

❧ From Gwinevere's Book of Shadows

November 21, 2002—Age 18

I have been reading reviews of my book *Spellcraft for Teens*. The majority of them are great, but one reviewer said something to the effect of, "A simple guide for Wicca newbies." From the rest of the review I could tell they weren't very receptive and I have this need to defend myself. Just because a book is basic, doesn't mean it's bad and just because someone is starting out on the path doesn't mean they should be labeled with a derogatory term. We all started at some point. Besides, being a beginner is only temporary! I am seriously against labels, and name-calling in general drives me nuts.

forward we could move in the right direction. There would be one less battle to fight, and have time to focus on more important issues facing the Wiccan/Pagan community.

Nature is neither good nor evil, though it is creative and destructive. Without death, there would be no life. Without darkness, there could be no light.
—Anubis RainHawk, age 15, California, USA

Male Practitioners

When I started compiling notes for *Confessions of a Teenage Witch* I knew that I wanted to write a different kind of book. Instead of suggesting you perform a ritual or circle casting I wrote, I'd offer a way to create one on your own. Instead of sharing my single point of view, I'd bring in other practitioners, opinions from around the world. And finally, instead of gearing it toward teen females like countless other metaphysical guides on the market, I would seek to reach both genders. Male practitioners, especially guys in their teens, have long been ignored by Wiccan authors. That oversight ends today. Within the next few pages you'll find information created for male teens to enhance and complement personal practice, tap into the power of dragons, and get in touch with your inner God.

Before we delve into the rituals, take a look at several contributors' views on practicing Wicca.

Male Wiccans are not taken seriously. Due to the inaccuracy of the media, many believe that Wiccans can only be female. Most books on the religion are written solely for female practitioners. Even worse, some publishers use the cover art on books to attract

the female readers, completely excluding the male practitioners. Many times, males are thought to have less power, due in part to the media. There are a wider variety of tools, books, and groups specifically for female Wiccans. It may take a while, but eventually the world will realize that male Wiccans exist, and are equal to female practitioners.
—ANUBIS RAINHAWK, AGE 15, CALIFORNIA, USA

I believe males get involved with the Craft to explore the sexual balance and learn of their feminine sides. They seek to develop their passivity to counteract the stereotypical active male.
—PYTHO, AGE 14, MILAN, ITALY

Males seek Wicca for the same reason women do—something calls us. When I first started researching Wicca, the concept of the Goddess, divinity in nature, and magick all seemed to fit. I was seeking answers, and seeking to experience the divine. Years later, I am practicing and still interested in this ancient spirituality. Both sexes can find answers within Wicca. That's why it's so diverse.
—ANUBIS RAINHAWK, AGE 15, CALIFORNIA, USA

Guys who follow Wicca are probably interested in finding out how they as individuals can learn to use their own sense of power and identity to make real changes and to affect their lives positively.
—GEDE, AGE 15, QUEENSLAND, AUSTRALIA

When a male Witch opens up about their Craft they are often met with skeptical and bemused looks, which seem to say, "You mean Warlock, right?" There could be nothing more aggravating; however it's not the public's fault that they don't realize that Witch is a term that can be applied to both genders.
—GEDE, AGE 15, QUEENSLAND, AUSTRALIA

The majority of books on Wicca empower women, but they sel-
dom realize that both sexes need empowerment.
—ANUBIS RAINHAWK, AGE 15, CALIFORNIA, USA

Working with Dragon Energy

Dragons are ancient and mythical creatures still honored in modern times as energy forms and kept alive through medieval and oriental folklore. Dragons were once believed to hold magical power, vitality and unearthly strength. As a symbol of good fortune, the dragon breathes new life and carries the winds of change on its wings.

Align your personal energy with these entities in their astral form by stirring (kindly awaking and inviting) them into your sacred space through the four elements. Below, you'll find dragon corner calls that I have developed. If you'd like, insert them in the circle casting format (step six) found in chapter Six. Some practitioners are weary about bringing dragon vibrations into the sacred space because they are thought to be very power-ful. However, it is my understanding that so long as they are stirred softly and given the utmost respect then dragons will be-come accustomed to the practitioner and benefit one's practice.

I love dragons and utilize their energy in my practice whenever
possible. Dragons are very powerful, magical creatures, and their
lives are infinite, making them wise consults.
—CHIRON NIGHTWOLF, AGE 16, GEORGIA, USA

Stand before the northern corner of your circle, hold up your preferred ritual tool, and speak this invocation:

> *"I stir power of sacred mysteries, Dragon of the majestic North.*
> *Awaken and come forth with heart of Earth,*
> *to watch over my rite and guard the gate between time.*
> *In your honor with perfect love and perfect trust. Blessed Be!"*

Visualize the dragon you are inviting to assist, standing on a fertile green field. Bow your head and move to the next element.

In front of the eastern corner of your circle, hold up your tool and say:

> *"I stir power of sacred mysteries, Dragon of the majestic East.*
> *Awaken and come forth with breath of Air,*
> *to watch over my rite and guard the gate between time.*
> *In your honor with perfect love and perfect trust. Blessed Be!"*

Visualize the dragon flying through the crisp, clean air. Bow your head and step to the next element.

Before the southern corner of your circle, hold up your tool and say:

> *"I stir power of sacred mysteries, Dragon of the majestic South.*
> *Awaken and come forth with spark of Fire,*
> *to watch over my rite and guard the gate between time.*
> *In your honor with perfect love and perfect trust. Blessed Be!"*

Visualize the dragon releasing a protective breath of fire. Bow your head and move on to the last element.

At the western corner of your circle, hold up your tool and say:

> *"I stir power of sacred mysteries, Dragon of the majestic West.*
> *Awaken and come forth with stream of Water,*

to watch over my rite and guard the gate between time.
In your honor with perfect love and perfect trust. Blessed Be!"

Visualize the dragon being cleansed in the soft rain. Bow your head and proceed with your circle casting and deity invocations.

To release these creatures (once you have completed your workings) stand before the western corner of your circle. Thank the water dragon for his help and bid him farewell. Bow your head and continue working clockwise, stopping at each of the corners and their respective elements.

GOD WITHIN RITUAL
This ritual draws upon the masculine form of divinity. It is written for male practitioners and focuses on the God in his solar aspect.

Supplies
One orange peel
Three cinnamon sticks
Two tablespoons chamomile
Small bowl

Additional Correspondences
Food: cashews, sesame sticks, sunflower seeds, walnuts
Drink: water, citrus juices (grapefruit, orange, pineapple, tangerine)
Incense: allspice, copal, frankincense, juniper, patchouli, sandalwood
Oils: bergamot, cedar, chamomile, cinnamon, juniper, orange, patchouli, rosemary, sandalwood

For best results, perform this ritual on a Sunday around noon.

After your circle has been cast, use the following invocation to invite the God. *Invoking the Goddess for this ritual is optional.*

"Bringer of dawn, ruler of day
Blazing God of solar illumination
He who is ancient
Ra, Sol, Lugh, Apollo
Lord of the Sun
I invite thee to my sacred space."

To begin, bring your supplies in front of you and sit comfortably. Close your eyes and visualize the warm sun. Imagine its rays coming into the room, dancing above your head, and softly streaming down your body. Continue to keep your eyes closed while you place your hands over the supplies. Feel the energy move through your arms, out your hands, and encompass the magickal items with God's light. When you're ready, open your eyes and proceed to the next step.

One by one combine the orange peel, cinnamon sticks and chamomile into the bowl. Immerse your hand into the mixture, feeling the citrus peel, herb, and spice. Recite the following incantation with passion.

"God, wild dancing spirit of fire
Lord, stream of golden light
He who is power
I take in your silken rays
and open my soul to your essence
guide me on my life's journey
I ask for your assistance
lend me your strength, perseverance, and wisdom
stir and awaken within me
so I may see the divine all around

shine down your love
show me your mysteries
God, wild dancing spirit of fire
Lord, stream of golden light
He who is power
show me the mysteries, for I am your son
Blessed Be!"

Remove your hand from the mixture and take a moment to reflect. Use the rest of your time to meditate, commune with deity, pray, or write in your Book of Shadows. If you'd like, partake in a small feast with food that corresponds to the God (see list above for suggestions). Afterwards, open your circle, clean up, and proceed with your afternoon.

Circle Casting

Wiccans cast a circle so we can open our mind, body, and spirit, connect with divinity, establish sacred space and prevent negative vibrations from disturbing our special workings. It also helps to achieve the desired ritual frame of mind—calm, receptive, intuitive, yet focused. The circle is created from the practitioner's personal energy, blessing of divinity, power of the four elements, as well as a physically defined and visualized psychic barrier.

This chapter will discuss in detail the twelve steps of circle casting. You'll be prompted to select from various options and express preferred methods, ultimately resulting in the creation of a personalized circle casting format. Upon completion of the exercises in this chapter, place a final version in your Book of Shadows.

Moving and crafting your energy into a cyclic pattern can help to arouse primal, instinctive emotions within the individual and

> ### ❧ From Gwinevere's Book of Shadows
> *June 16, 1999—Age 14*
> I had a vivid dream about an old room filled with Wicca, Goddess, and magick books. The bookcases were against a wall, covering it from floor to ceiling. The sun shined through several tall windows as I stood in the center of a circle. I felt that I was in a sacred place.

induce trancelike states. So many things in nature and in the universe move in circular paths or cycles and so as we mime the lull of nature's way we are merging the sun, the moon, the seasons, the worlds, and humanity into one concentrated pulse of living, vibrant energy.
—GEDE, AGE 15, QUEENSLAND, AUSTRALIA

When I am performing rituals or hosting gatherings of a group of Witches, I will cast a magick circle and say a small blessing, if only to balance the energies in the room.
—CHIRON NIGHTWOLF, AGE 16, GEORGIA, USA

Preparations

WHERE TO CASTE?
One of the first issues you'll want to address before delving into circle casting is where you'd like to set up your sacred space. As teens we are somewhat limited in our options. Traditional Wiccans suggest practicing outside in order to be with nature and connect with divinity. However, most backyards don't provide enough privacy for such a venture. Working rituals and spells inside do have their benefits: no concerns over the weather, intrigued

neighbors, or wind blowing out candles. Indoors you might have the opportunity to cast the circle in the living room, but most teens opt for the bedroom. This is probably where you keep your tools, spell ingredients, and altar, so it makes sense to practice where you're most comfortable, have access to your supplies, and can maintain a reasonable degree of privacy. If your heart is set on being with nature, take a small walk before you settle down to cast your circle. Breathe in the fresh air, feel the energy of nature, then return inside to work your ritual or spell. For more information on when to cast spells and perform rituals see chapter Ten.

> *When I am doing a ritual indoors, I almost always cast a circle. When I'm out in the woods, I usually don't feel I need the circle because nature is sacred the way it is.*
> —LUNA, AGE 16, FINLAND

WHAT TO WEAR?

Practitioners have three clothing options: working skyclad (in the nude), adorning special ritual garb such as a robe, cape, favorite outfit, renaissance dress, etc., or wearing casual everyday clothing (my personal choice). I've always believed that the higher powers care more about a practitioner's inner spirit, love, and positive intentions than what he or she may (or may not) be wearing. If you're unsure of which choice is right for you, give them each a try to find out. Remember, it's all about doing what feels most comfortable. Wearing jewelry with significant meaning or symbolism can also add to your experience. Donning a pentacle necklace is a common (but optional) practice.

> *It is solely the decision of the individual to decide whether to practice nude or clothed. Personally, I think working skyclad is better because it brings you back to your natural form.*
> —ANUBIS RAINHAWK, AGE 15, CALIFORNIA, USA

I have never practiced skyclad, mostly because the thought of my little sister barging in unexpectedly scares me.
—LYNX SONG, AGE 15, LOUISIANA, USA

PRIVACY

Rituals, spells, holidays, and full moons each have a significant role in Wicca. We use these formats and methods to connect with divinity, feel empowered, and attain our goals. It is important that rituals are not rushed through or interrupted. Privacy and the right environment are essential. Planning ahead of time can help avoid time constraints or disturbances. Reflect for a moment and think of a time when family members are occupied, perhaps watching TV at night or when siblings are visiting the mall on a weekend. Explain that you would like time alone in your room to hang out, meditate, or partake in "Wicca stuff." With the right mind-set and a bit of scheduling, you can achieve privacy and a peaceful circle casting.

MISC. PREPARATIONS

My average ritual is about forty-five minutes, so I try to get as comfortable as possible. When sitting before lit candles I make sure to tie my hair back—it is a quick and necessary precaution. Slipping off my shoes is another pre-ritual step. It shows respect to the higher powers and sanctifies sacred space. Lastly, since the circle is a "place between time," I take off my watch and turn away the clock in my room. This allows me to temporarily forget about the outer world, its stress, and demands, and reflect on the true meaning of my ritual's focus.

ANTICIPATE PROBLEMS

Even with the best planning, sometimes you forget a much-needed tool, accidentally spill your Full Moon–blessed water, or get interrupted by a family member. What can you do? Get upset, or deal with the situation. Anticipating a problem ahead of time will help you maintain focus, fix the issue quickly, and proceed instead of losing the desire to continue. The following is a list of potential problems you may encounter along with helpful tips on how to combat them.

Clumsy? Tuck a paper towel in the back of your Book of Shadows. In the event of a spill, it will be easy to access.

Forget a tool? First, consider how much the implement will be needed. Pointing your index finger can substitute for a misplaced wand or athame. Alternatively, use visualization to cut a door, walk out, grab the missing item, and return inside your circle, sealing it closed. This prevents it from feeling broken or disturbed.

Interrupted by a family member knocking on your door? Take a moment to decide what to do, depending on the situation. If need be, close up the circle and return later to finish the ritual or spell.

The Twelve Steps of Circle Casting

STEP ONE: RITUAL MOOD
Creating a serene atmosphere will have a calming effect and aid in ritual focus. There are three ways to set the ambiance: self-purification, easy lighting, and soft music. Some practitioners suggest taking a purification bath; to conserve time, rinse your hands and face under flowing water or anoint your third eye and wrists with Full Moon–blessed water. Whichever method you choose, visualize negativity draining away.

For lighting effects, candles are preferred. However, a twenty-five-watt bulb in a lamp across the room will also offer enough light to read your Book of Shadows without being too overwhelming or bright. For an extra touch look for color-tinted "party lightbulbs," which come in special colors!

Listening to a soothing CD set on a low volume while performing a ritual or spell may contribute positively to the ritual mood. There are many choices including but not limited to: sounds of the ocean, rhythmic chanting, Goddess songs, Enya, Celtic theme, or classical music.

✤ From Gwinevere's Book of Shadows

June 4, 2003—Age 18

Right now it's thundering. The sound rumbles, radiating throughout the house. I love the sound of a good summer storm. The crackling of the thunder rolls underneath my feet. My connection to the earth seems to expand during storms. Some of my best magick has been cast during rain showers, thunderstorms, and cozy nighttime silence. The weather sets the mood tonight as much as the candle flames dancing on my altar.

STEP TWO: SETUP

When laying out the circle, you'll want to make sure there is enough room to walk around, easily access your tools, sit comfortably, and set up a small working area. For a solitary practitioner the average circle is about four to six feet in diameter. The more people that join the space, the bigger it should be. To define the physical aspect of your circle place a lengthy ribbon or cord on the ground in a rough circular shape. Other ways to define sacred space include arranging stones, shells, flower petals, pinecones, or a circle drawn in chalk.

Your working area will be limited in space so a small portable altar (like a food tray) can be used. I place my deity representations along with the ritual/spell supplies on a portable altar tray. I then place my wand, broom, and Book of Shadows to my side.

Next, select your element representations (see section in chapter Four) and place them in their respective directions: North/earth, East/air, South/fire, and West/water inside the circle. Double-check to make sure you have all the necessary tools and supplies for your ritual or spell. To make sure I don't forget any important tools or supplies, I create a checklist on a piece of scrap paper and mark items off as I include them in my sacred space.

In your Book of Shadows record how you intend to define the circle, create a working area, and which element representations you've decided upon.

STEP THREE: CLEANSE SACRED SPACE

There are several methods to cleanse sacred space but the goal remains the same: banishing negativity and purifying the area for ritual purposes. I use my broom to sweep the circle and cast away unwanted energies. Visit the tool section in chapter Four for more detailed instructions. Burning incense or sage bundles are additional options to cleanse sacred space. The practitioner walks *deosil* (clockwise), visualizing the area being purified and released of negativity.

Salt water is an additional consecration method. Add a few pinches of salt to a jar of fresh water and infuse with positive energy. The empowered mixture can then be used in one of two ways: Coat fresh rosemary, mint, or sage sprigs in the salt water and then asperges (sprinkle) the circle, softly moving *deosil*. Or, dip two to three fingers in the mixture and flick the water around the circle's circumference. For each of the methods

Sage and rosemary bundles for cleansing sacred space.

discussed above a blessing can be said or chanted to affirm the process. Remember, visualize and work in a clockwise fashion.

Use your Book of Shadows to express which purification method you intend to use and write a blessing to go along with the creation of sacred space.

STEP FOUR: CENTER

The purpose of centering is to help release pent-up negativity and achieve a ritual mind frame. What follows is my basic format. Feel free to adapt it to suit your needs.

To begin, stand in the middle of your circle and face North. Place your feet firmly on the ground in line with your shoulders. Keep your arms to your sides or stretch them up high, palms open (this is referred to as the Goddess Position). If you intend on using a wand or athame to cast your circle, you may want to hold it in your power hand (the one you write with) during this exercise.

Close your eyes and take deep breaths, inhaling through your nose and slowly exhaling through your mouth. Clear your mind of lingering thoughts and visualize your feet as part of the earth; perhaps see them as roots. Link your whole body to Mother Earth and draw up her positive energy in the form of a visualized white or green mist. Pull up her powerful, loving vibrations and let them sink into every part of your being.

After a few moments, visualize your feet as they truly are and focus on your breath. Once your breathing is back to normal, slowly open your eyes. If you were in the Goddess Position, let your arms fall to your sides and proceed to cast your circle.

Use your Book of Shadows to make notes on this centering exercise. Will you hold your wand or athame? Will you stand in the Goddess Position or keep your hands down? How would you change the visualization to suit your needs?

Standard Wiccan rituals such as casting the circle are not always the highest on my list of priorities. I find that simply focusing and centering my mind before a magickal working is something that suits my purpose far better.
—GEDE, AGE 15, QUEENSLAND, AUSTRALIA

I always cast a circle at Sabbats and Esbats, but if I am doing "lesser" magick I will often simply say a prayer of protection before doing my work.
—ARIAWN, AGE 19, OHIO, USA

STEP FIVE: CREATE A CIRCLE OF ENERGY
This step is an integral part of casting the circle, so work slowly, with a focused mind. Use the open palm of your power hand, wand, or athame to aid in this task. To begin, stand before the Northern corner, holding out your palm or tool directly in line

with the edge of your circle. Close your eyes and draw in energy from the air surrounding you; visualize divine power from the moon, sun, and earth seeping into your arm. Open your eyes and project the energy through your arm, down your hand, into your tool, and out onto the circle's circumference. Visualize this stream of energy in the form of light, mist, or sparks.

Keep your palm or tool aligned with the circle while you turn to your side and slowly start to walk around the sacred space in a clockwise manner. Continue to project the visualized energy passing each of the other elements: air, fire, and water. Finally when you return to the earth element in the North, seal the circle and pull your hand (wand or athame) toward your chest. Speak an incantation affirming the creation of your circle.

In your Book of Shadows detail each step you'll take when creating a circle of energy. Will you use your power hand, wand, or athame? How will you visualize the projected energy: in the form of light, mist, or sparks? Will you "see" a specific color? Do you want your circle to be a ring, whole barrier, sphere, or dome? Also, create an incantation to speak once the circle of energy has been formed.

> *It feels like your aura is expanded five feet around you, and the world just seems to crumble away. The space inside the circle seems surrealistic—like a dreamtime or walking on clouds. Despite the dreamy atmosphere, your mind becomes focused and balanced.*
> —PYTHO, AGE 14, MILAN, ITALY

> *When casting a circle, it is like building a barrier in the shape of a sphere that makes that space both part of this world and the divine. It feels almost supercharged, and I sense a light pressure when I get close to the edges. It is warm.*
> —ARIAWN, AGE 19, OHIO, USA

STEP SIX: INVOKE THE ELEMENTS

In the circle each of the elements are linked to one of the four cardinal points. North is associated with earth, East to air, South to fire, and West to water. The combination of elements and directions are called corners, guardians, or watchtowers. Individually invoked and invited we draw upon their energy to oversee our workings, contribute power, and prevent negativity from entering sacred space. Some Wiccans also choose to invoke angels, elementals, or dragons but this is a completely optional and personalized practice.

To invite the four corners, the process involves action, visualization, and spoken prayer. Most traditions start at North, which is considered to be the direction of power. Others start in the East, where both the sun and moon rise. Once you've decided upon a direction, visualize the attributes associated with the particular element: North is nurturing, nourishing, fertile, and green. Feel the power within you, hold up your wand or athame and point it toward the chosen corner, and speak a firm, yet respectful invocation.

At this point, some practitioners draw what is called an "invoking pentagram" (upright star) in the air with their preferred tool. Continue your visualization through the invocation, wait a moment, then slowly lower your tool and move on to the next corner. Repeat the process once again for the next corner using the proper imagery and element associations.

Using your Book of Shadows, write down invocations for each element. Determine if you'd like to work with other entities (angels, elements, dragons, totem animals, etc.). Make notes on visualizing each element and decide if you'll draw the invoking pentagram.

When casting a circle, I feel each of the individual elements entering the circle: the strength and comfort of earth, the knowledge

and wisdom of air, the energy and power of fire, and the emo-
tional, motherly caress of water.
—CHIRON NIGHTWOLF, AGE 16, GEORGIA, USA

STEP SEVEN: INVOKE THE GODDESS AND GOD

Wiccans invoke the Goddess and God to witness sacred rituals, as well as aid in protection and bless magical workings. Each time the deity is invoked, the further you connect with and attune to their energies. In many ways, you are also awakening a divine spark—the Goddess and God within. Write your own invocations from the heart or use pre-written ones from other sources. Visit chapter Three for my prayers and invocations.

Whether you are borrowing an invocation from a book or writing your own, remember to use visualization. The invites can be as general or specific as you'd like. To begin the invocation process, sit comfortably and look to your deity representations. Focus on the energy of the Goddess and God.

Slowly begin reading the invocation, taking in each word and meaningful symbolism. Think of a forest with a running stream, wild animals, shooting stars, ripening fruit, warm comforting arms, and a welcoming smile. Truly believe that their loving vibrations are present. You might even feel a subtle change in the circle's atmosphere.

Use your Book of Shadows to record invocations, visualizations, and other notes for inviting the higher powers.

STEP EIGHT: PERFORM RITUAL OR SPELL

Circles are cast to help the practitioner focus on their workings. These workings include but are not limited to: Sabbats, Full Moon rites, meaningful rituals, magick spells, prolonged meditation, divination, spiritual quests/exercises, or communing with divinity. You workings should be prepared in advance so as

> ❧ From Gwinevere's Book of Shadows
> *February 16, 2000—Age 15*
> It occurred to me, when I invoke the Goddess and God, I take it quite
> seriously. I think there is a line between asking for their presence and
> begging. Even if my ritual task is serious, it feels wrong to lower myself
> by making some desperate plea. I find other ways to emphasize my
> need, by saying things like, "Lord and Lady, this is important to me, I
> would appreciate your guidance and support." It is my belief that when
> using proper invocations, respect becomes mutual.

not to forget any special tools or supplies. Remember to focus, visualize, have fun, and harm none.

> *I like the feeling inside the circle. The circle is not only a sacred*
> *space between worlds; it offers protection and healing energy.*
> *When working with spells, the circle magnifies the energy and*
> *makes the spell more powerful.*
> —Anubis RainHawk, age 15, California, USA

STEP NINE: GROUND
Grounding releases pent-up energy raised during a ritual or
spell. It is sent into the earth, returning your body to a natural,
less excited state. Optimally after grounding you'll feel relaxed
and refreshed. There are two ways to "earth the power": partaking in a ritual feast (also called cakes and wine/cakes and ale) or
performing a quick mediation exercise.

While the word *feast* may conjure up images of Thanksgiv-
ing dinner, for ritual it is more symbolic. The chalice is filled
with water or juice (see chalice information in chapter Four for

---

❧ From Gwinevere's Book of Shadows

September 10, 2003—Age 19

I was completely there—my heart, mind, body, and soul. I cast two spells and participated in a Full Moon rite. Alone at my altar I sat, my Book of Shadows close by with detailed layout and instructions. I had planned for this for days. Beforehand I was nervous. Was it the spell's topic? Or that I hadn't cast a circle in months? I don't know what it was exactly, but I told myself to channel the energy, tap into it, use the power toward my goals. Once I cast the circle, invoked my deities and corners, things felt familiar. Almost like living a memory again. Words, actions similar, a recognition of sacred space.

---

seasonal suggestions) and the food consists of a piece of fruit, muffin, cookies, or crackers. Prior to circle casting, the snacks are placed on a napkin and then onto an altar pentacle for blessing and consecration purposes.

For fewer tools and less fuss, try the following grounding technique: Sit (or lie down) with your palms open flat beside you, touching the floor. Take deep calming breaths, inhaling through your nose and exhaling through your mouth. Concentrate on your breathing for a moment. Next, visualize pulsating energy moving through your arms, out your palms, and into the ground. Allow any negative thoughts or doubts to travel with the flow. When you're ready, picture a cool, white mist coming up from the earth's core into your palms. Allow this light to fill your whole body with calm and peaceful vibrations.

Using your Book of Shadows, convey your preferred grounding method. Will you partake in the ritual feast or meditation exercise? Are there any parts of the technique you'd like to personalize?

Step Ten: Thank the Goddess and God

At this point in the circle casting process you'll bid farewell to the energies that were previously invited, starting with the Goddess and God. Since divinity is around us all the time to guide and protect, this step is more of a formal gesture than firm "good-bye." Your closing statement can be prepared ahead of time or improvised on the spot. Thank them for aiding and overseeing your ritual, for their presence, comfort, and love, as well as the daily blessings they send. Words have power, so be sure to speak with kindness and respect. Divinity isn't meant to be "dismissed."

The comments can be as simple or complex as you'd like. An example to work from: "Depart with love, you're always in my heart, Merry Part and Blessed Be." If you're using candles as your deity representations, extinguish them as you speak your farewell message. An offering of thanks such as a seashell, dried flower, artwork, or something handcrafted can also be presented.

Utilizing your Book of Shadows, write your ideas and comments on this step. Will your farewell be impromptu or pre-written? Include your message in your Book if you intend to have one prepared ahead of time. Will you make any gestures (such as extinguishing a candle) or include an offering?

Step Eleven: Release the Elements

Releasing the elements is similar to thanking the Goddess and God. Remember to be respectful and appreciative. Your farewell can be scripted or thought up on the spot. Practitioners usually work widdershins (counterclockwise) to dismantle the circle so start at West/water, proceed to South/fire, East/air, and finally North/earth. If you drew an invoking pentagram in step Six you'll need to draw a banishing pentagram to release each element. To do this, start at the bottom-right point and draw the pentagram in the opposite fashion. It helps to practice using pen and paper to get accustomed to the motion.

Use your Book of Shadows to write your thoughts on scripted versus on-the-spot farewell comments. Create a small note for yourself to perform a banishing pentagram if you previously drew an invoking pentagram.

STEP TWELVE: OPEN THE CIRCLE

To return the area to its normal state, you'll want to use the three methods used in step Five (creating a circle of energy) to visualize, perform an action, and create a verbalized statement.

Stand in the center of your circle and hold up your hand, wand or athame toward the sky. Move your hand or tool clockwise in the air above your head, creating a full circle. Speak a closing incantation as you point to the ground with your hand or tool. Visualize the circle as a mist falling and disappearing into the earth. As an alternative, you may want to walk along the circle's circumference, drawing the energy into a tool for future workings.

Detail your ideas for opening the circle in your Book of Shadows. Include an incantation and how you'd like to disperse the energy, whether into the earth or into a ritual tool.

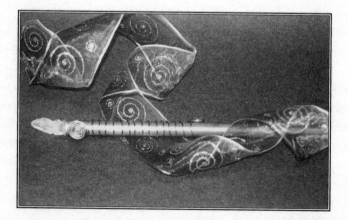

SEVEN

The Sabbats

The Wiccan Sabbats are made up of eight sacred holidays and intertwine to create the Wheel of the Year. Our modern-day Sabbats are comprised of seasonal transitions and Celtic festivals. The two solstices and two equinoxes divide the year into four quarters: winter, spring, summer, and fall. The Celtic festivals Imbolc, Beltane, Lughnasadh, and Samhain occur on fixed dates between these seasonal points.

Wiccans honor the Wheel of the Year to connect with nature and Her cycle, but also to learn the mythic story of the Goddess and God. Each Sabbat contains a small part of this story and reflects the theme of either birth, life, death, or regeneration. Symbolism is woven into every holiday: whatever happens to the sun and its natural transitions affects the God's journey.

The Wiccan Wheel of the Year

Yule (Winter Solstice) *around* December 21st
Imbolc celebrated on February 2nd
Ostara (Vernal Equinox) *around* March 21st
Beltane celebrated on April 30th
Litha (Summer Solstice) *around* June 21st
Lughnasadh celebrated on August 1st
Mabon (Autumn Equinox) *around* September 21st
Samhain celebrated on October 31st

The solstice and equinox dates vary year to year. For example, the winter solstice (Yule) can occur anywhere from December 20th to the 23rd. It's a good idea to check your calender for the specific date.

Sabbats are festive occasions that mark specific passages experienced by the eternal Goddess and the living God. Each is a celebration of one aspect of the journey of life—life, death, and Rebirth. Celebrating and honoring these events with others is a fun and beautiful thing. Generally I celebrate the Sabbats with close friends or a slightly larger group.
—GEDE, AGE 15, QUEENSLAND, AUSTRALIA

I'm fascinated by the power involved during the equinoxes. On those days, light and dark are in balance, which also help to bring balance to my own spirit.
—PYTHO, AGE 14, MILAN, ITALY

Although many Wiccans consider the start of the Sabbats to be Samhain or Yule, the Wheel of the Year is a continuous cycle; you can begin your journey at any time. Some practitioners celebrate together coven style, others find meaning in solitary work. A Sabbat can be informal—meditating and reflecting on the holiday, or performing something slightly more complex like reciting a poem while lighting a candle in sacred space.

In this chapter you'll find Sabbat descriptions, correspondences, and ritual concepts. Utilize these notes as a foundation for creating your own rituals. It's best to cast a circle but ultimately the choice is up to you. Also, feel free to expand on my suggestions. For example, you'll notice colors listed for each holiday. Consider implementing those colors for candles, altar cloths, ribbons, or other altar decorations. Remember to keep finished rituals in your Book of Shadows for future use.

> *I prefer simple rituals, in which I give thanks for the season, and sometimes lay out flowers depending on the time of year.*
> —CHIRON NIGHTWOLF, AGE 16, GEORGIA, USA

> *After casting my circle, I invoke a certain aspect of the Goddess and/or God. I take out the lore I've found on the Sabbat and read it. I try to meditate on what I've read and connect with the Sabbat. Then, my favorite part, I write a poem about the Sabbat and dedicate it to the Goddess or the God. After thanking the deities, I dismantle the circle, date the poem, and put it in a special part of my Book of Shadows.*
> —LYNX SONG, AGE 15, LOUISIANA, USA

Yule

The winter solstice falls on or around December 21st and occurs when the sun is at one degree Capricorn. Each winter solstice marks the birth of the God from the Goddess and is the longest night of the year.

Food and Drink: Eggnog, spiced tea, gingerbread, fruit-cake, sugar cookies, cranberries, dried fruits, nuts.

Herbs and Flowers: Pine needles, pinecones, holly, mistletoe, juniper, ivy, cedar, bay, cloves, rosemary, nutmeg, cinnamon, ginger, valerian, myrrh.

Colors: Red, green, white.

YULE SABBAT CONCEPTS

- Write a poem or incantation to mark the Sabbat. Recite during Yule ritual in sacred space.

- Decorate the family Christmas/Yule tree with handmade ornaments or string Victorian style—garland made of cranberries and popcorn.

- Read classic holiday stories to younger siblings or cousins.

- Say a blessing over holiday treats while baking for future happiness and well-being.

- Light a candle, place in a safe holder, and walk it around a sacred space (in a clockwise motion) to symbolize the turning of the wheel of the year.

- Create a miniature wreath with ribbons, evergreens, and strings of gold beads. Place above your altar. Supplies can be purchased beforehand at your local craft store.

- Put out holiday cards from long-distance family members who can't join you during this festive time.

- Create images of the sun, bless and display on altar as an offering.

Altar Decorations: A poinsettia plant, mistletoe, holly, pinecones, bells, candy canes, solar images.

Advanced Craft: Make a gingerbread house. Use graham crackers, white icing, and gumdrops.

> *Yule is a special time that helps me to look forward to the rebirth of the Lord and the Earth, and it is also very close to my own birthday.*
> —ARIAWN, AGE 19, OHIO, USA

❧ From Gwinevere's Book of Shadows

December 23, 1999—Age 15

Yesterday, I had a Yule celebration with my mom. We lit a fire, burned old papers to start the year fresh, and toasted marshmallows. It wasn't a traditional Wicca celebration, but it turned out to be something special.

Imbolc

This is celebrated on February 2nd. It is known as the time which the Goddess recovers from childbirth and the earth is renewing itself from a long winter's slumber. This is a time of purification and inspiration. Imbolc is also known as Oimelc, Brigid, or Candlemas.

Food and Drink: Honey, raisins, spicy foods, hot soups, milk, cheese, other dairy foods.

Herbs and Flowers: Pine needles, pinecones, holly, juniper, ivy, willow, rowan, mint, rosemary, dill.

Colors: Silver, white, deep green.

IMBOLC SABBAT CONCEPTS

- Write a poem or incantation in honor of the Sabbat. Recite during Imbolc ritual in sacred space.

- Snuggle the bottom of a white candle in a bowl or cauldron filled with earth. Light the wick and say a prayer to the recovering Goddess.

- Sprinkle white flower petals in a circle pattern on your altar while visualizing the wheel of the year turning.

- Help banish winter by melting ice in a bowl or burning paper-shaped snowflakes.

- Bless seeds for fruitfulness and bounty. Plant when warm weather comes.

Altar Decorations: Evergreens, clear quartz, white flowers, white candles, symbolic snowflakes, jar of milk.

Advanced Craft: Make a corn doll by weaving corn husks into a female figure to symbolize the Goddess.

Ostara

The vernal equinox falls on or around March 21st and occurs when the sun is at one degree Aries. On this first day of spring, the hours of night and day are equal, the God nears maturity, and fertility is abound with new floral and animal life. Ostara is alternatively spelled as Oestara.

Food and Drink: Eggs, honey, biscuits, hot cross buns, vanilla cupcakes, sunflower seeds, spring salad with green leafy vegetables.

Herbs and Flowers: Dogwood, daffodil, honeysuckle, woodruff, violet, peony, iris, narcissus, crocus, jasmine, primrose, Irish moss, ginger.

Colors: Pastel shades of pink, yellow, green, blue.

Ostara Sabbat Concepts

- Write a poem or incantation to mark the Sabbat. Recite during Ostara ritual in sacred space.

- Dye hard-boiled eggs, paying special attention to the colors. Green represents growth/money; pink—love; purple—psychic enhancement; yellow—friendship and joy. When the eggs have dried, keep in fridge till ritual. In sacred space, bless the egg with your magical intention. While eating, visualize your desired outcome.

- Take a walk in nature and say a prayer of thanks for your many blessings.

- Brush up on floral lore and their magical properties.

- Incorporate edible seeds like sunflower or sesame into your ritual. With each one you eat, invite spring change into your life.

- Gift chocolate eggs to family and friends as a sign of thoughtfulness.

- Plant flowers and herbs while speaking a magical chant for growth and abundance.

Altar Decorations: Representations (statues, pictures) of spring life; yellow chicks, bunnies, baby birds and animals. Pastel-shaded flowers, white craft feathers, bundles of fresh-cut grass, Ostara/Easter candy such as robin's eggs, marshmallow bunnies. Foods that symbolize fertility; eggs, nuts, or seeds.

Advanced Craft: Start a small potted garden. Keep in your bedroom on the windowsill.

🌿 From Gwinevere's Book of Shadows

March 20, 2002—Age 17

Ostara is the kind of Sabbat that makes me feel like a kid again. Everywhere I go this time of the year there are pastel decorations and images of smiling bunny posters. I think of being little during Easter, hunting for plastic eggs filled with candy then sitting on the couch surrounded by wrapped treats. It's also one of the only times of the year people actually stop to consider nature's cycle, this time of new birth and earths reawakening.

Beltane

Celebrated on April 30th, this Sabbat signifies the height of fertility for the Goddess, while the God reaches adulthood. Their symbolic union (marriage and mating) ends in conception, brings forth new life, further growth, and a continuation of the wheel of the year cycle. Beltane is also known as May Day and alternatively spelled as Bealtaine.

> Food and Drink: cherries, strawberries, cheese, milk, vanilla ice cream, oatmeal cookies.
>
> Herbs and Flowers: hawthorn, honeysuckle, woodruff, primrose, rose, birch, rosemary, lilac.
>
> Colors: Green, blue, deep pink, violet.

BELTANE SABBAT CONCEPTS

- Write a poem or incantation in honor of the Sabbat. Recite during Beltane ritual in sacred space.

- Gather fresh flowers to simulate a wedding bouquet.

- Tie rings with white ribbon to symbolize the Goddess and God's handfasting.

- Weave brightly colored ribbons together to represent a mini Maypole.

- Plunge athame into chalice to symbolize the "great rite," unity of the Goddess and God.

- Incorporate artistic ventures in ritual and dedicate your end product to the Lord and Lady.

Altar Decorations: Butterfly images (which represent transformation), fresh-scented flowers, colorful ribbons, symbols of unity.

Advanced Craft: Make a headpiece with craft flowers and ribbons. Wear during Beltane ritual.

> *I really like Beltane because it celebrates life, the earth, and the union of the Goddess and God. At Beltane, the earth flourishes and the love of the God and Goddess is seen in all life.*
> —ANUBIS RAINHAWK, AGE 15, CALIFORNIA, USA

> *Beltane is a favorite because of the vibrancy of the season, and if you inhale deep and slow as soon as you walk outside you can smell the love, fertility, and sweetness in the air. It just makes me thankful to be alive.*
> —ARIAWN, AGE 19, OHIO, USA

Litha

The Summer Solstice falls on or around June 21st when the sun is at one degree Cancer. Litha is celebrated on the longest day of the year and is a time of great magical energy. The God reaches his prime and his symbol, the sun, is at its peak. The Goddess (Earth Mother) is pregnant with the God and nature's bounty. Litha is also known as Midsummer.

Food and Drink: Lemonade, peaches, apricots, oranges, grapefruit, summer berries, yellow squash, hot and spicy foods.

Herbs and Flowers: Sunflower, chamomile, ginger, rose, lily, lavender, daisy, carnation, ivy, elder, frankincense, sandalwood, mugwort, yarrow, vervain, mint, fennel, thyme.

Colors: gold, bright yellow, bright orange, bright pink.

LITHA SABBAT CONCEPTS

- Write a poem or incantation to mark the Sabbat. Recite during Litha ritual in sacred space.

- Empower and light an orange or yellow candle. Wave your hand over the flame away from you to banish negative influences and then back toward you for purification. This action is symbolic of balefire jumping.

- Use a mirror to capture the sunlight or a candle flame.

- Float flower-shaped candles in a bowl or cauldron of water.

- Gather and dry herbs for fall and winter stock.

- Work spells for love, health, prosperity, and protection. Litha is a great peak of magical energy.

Altar Decorations: Fairy offerings, charms, or tokens, solar symbols, mirror, gold ribbons or beads, orange flowers, such as marigolds.

Advanced Craft: Make a sunwheel: Take two fallen branches of equal length, cross over to form a "T" shape and tie together. Decorate with orange and yellow paint, ribbons, and/or beads. The sunwheel represents the two solstices and equinoxes, and makes a great altar decoration. Bless within sacred space and incorporate into ritual.

All Sabbats are wonderful, as they are each different. They have their own characteristics and help me to tune in with the seasons

and the cycle of the year. Summer Sabbats are nice, because it's warm. I can practice outside and get fresh vegetables and berries.
—LUNA, AGE 16, FINLAND

Lughnasadh

Celebrated on August 1st, this Sabbat marks the beginning of the harvest. As fall approaches and the hours of sunlight begin to wane, the God starts to lose his strength. The Goddess realizes that He is dying but is also living inside of Her womb. Lughnasadh is also known as Lammas.

Food and Drink: Cornbread, rye bread, grapes, summer berries, peaches, apricots, oatmeal cookies, pretzels, wheat crackers, red juice.

Herbs and Flowers: Grains, heather, acorns, acacia flowers, myrtle, sunflower, poppies, sandalwood, chamomile, sage, ginger, galangal.

Colors: corn-yellow, gold, deep orange, red.

LUGHNASADH SABBAT CONCEPTS

- Write a poem or incantation in honor of the Sabbat. Recite during Lughnasadh ritual in sacred space.

- Bury an apricot or peach pit in a bowl of dirt during your ritual to symbolically represent the God's approaching descent into the underworld.

- Take a meditative walk in the evening to see the sun set as you reflect on the passing of summer.

- Fill a large seashell with dried oats to represent the first harvest.

- Place the head of a fresh sunflower on a simple white dish, sprinkle Indian corn (multicolored dried corn) around the flower. Use during your ritual as a symbol of energy and joy.

Altar Decorations: Oats, sunflowers, corn, grains, popcorn kernels, fragrant herbal sachets, deep orange–colored candles.

Advanced Craft: Make fresh bread. While mixing and kneading, infuse with positive energy and say a magical blessing.

❧ From Gwinevere's Book of Shadows

August 1, 2001—Age 16

Lughnasadh is one of my favorite holidays because it is a great time of personal reflection. My birthday is in a few days, and the summer afternoon is hot, but peaceful. Yet, I know fall will be here soon and envelop the yard with crisp leaves. Not to forget of course, that Lughnasada brings some of the best strawberries and peaches of the year.

Mabon

The autumnal equinox falls on or around September 21st, when the sun is at one degree Libra. On this first day of fall, the hours of night and day are equal, the second harvest is celebrated, and the earth readies for the approaching cold. The God gets closer to the veil of the underworld and the Goddess begins to mourn his loss. Mabon is also known as Harvest Home.

Food and Drink: Cornbread, nuts, grapes, cranberries, raspberries, pears, apples, vegetables (corn, carrots, potatoes, beans, onion) apple juice or cider, apple pie

Herbs and Flowers: Acorns, pinecones, heather, rose hips, yarrow, cinnamon, sage, star anise, patchouli, hawthorn, hazel, ivy, cedar.

Colors: Brown, burnt orange, maroon.

MABON SABBAT CONCEPTS

- Write a poem or incantation to mark the Sabbat. Recite during Mabon ritual in sacred space.

- Collect and sprinkle autumn leaves on your altar to signify the first day of fall.

- Make candied apples with caramel. Infuse them with positive energy. Give to loved ones and enjoy as a special treat.

- Weave black and white ribbons together to mark the balance of equal day and night.

- Add dried apple seeds to a mojo bag (cloth sachet) with yarrow and patchouli for a fragrant fall charm.

- Find a fallen leaf, hold it between your palms, bless it with healing energy. Release it outside while standing in the wind as a thanks to Mother Earth.

Altar Decorations: Symbols of balance (ying yang), acorns, mini pumpkins, gourds, nut shells, autumn leaves, brown or maroon candles.

Advanced Craft: Make a cornucopia (horn of plenty). Fill with apples, pears, nuts, and grapes as a symbol of prosperity and abundance.

Samhain

Celebrated on October 31st, this is a time when the separation between our earthly plane and the spiritual realm is at its thinnest. The God descends into the underworld, but His spirit lives in the Goddess and awaits rebirth at Yule. This sacred night marks the Celtic New Year and plays a significant role in the God's mythic cycle of death and regeneration. Samhain is also known as All Hallows' Eve and Halloween.

Food and Drink: Apple juice or cider, pumpkin pie, pumpkin bread, squash, gourds, corn, apples, pears, pomegranates, grains, nuts.

Herbs and Flowers: Mugwort, sage, allspice, catnip, chrysanthemum, marigolds, wormwood, hazel, thistle, rosemary, thyme.

Colors: black, orange.

SAMHAIN SABBAT CONCEPTS

- Write a poem or incantation in honor of the Sabbat. Recite during Samhain ritual in sacred space.

- Make a sun image out of paper and bury it in a bowl of dirt to symbolically represent the death of the God.

- Cut open a red apple and eat half, savoring its fresh taste. Save the other half to leave outside for the deceased.

- On a piece of paper, write your regrets, emotional hurts, and spiritual pains. Light the paper on fire and toss it in a fireproof cauldron (or empty coffee can) to release the past.

- Say a prayer in honor of loved ones who have passed.

- Sweep ritual area with ritual broom to banish the past and make a clean start for the new year.

- Samhain is an optimal time to partake in divination, past-life recall or other psychic endeavors.

Altar Decorations: Mini pumpkins, gourds, apples, pictures of deceased loved ones (pets, too!), orange or black candles, autumn leaves.

Advanced Craft: Make a jack-o'-lantern. Carve out a medium-sized pumpkin (setting inner membrane and seeds aside), make cuts for eyes, nose, and mouth. When it's done, place a tealight candle inside the pumpkin, light, and place outside to ward off evil spirits.

> *Samhain reminds us of death and the mysterious. The veil between worlds is thinnest as the God descends into the underworld. It is a time to recognize our ancestors, other realms, and our life's path.*
> —ANUBIS RAINHAWK, AGE 15, CALIFORNIA, USA

EIGHT

The Full Moon

I n this chapter we'll focus on the full moon and its place in Wiccan practice. As the most influential and celebrated phase it is a special time to focus on the feminine aspect of divinity. Through ritual we seek to establish a deeper connection with the Goddess and honor Her luminous qualities of love, light, and protection. During these ceremonies practitioners draw upon pulsating energy that affects the human body and ocean tides as a catalyst to put our goals in motion. The full moon is a scared time nestled within each month for reverence, worship, magick, and mystery.

On this night . . .

- Covens are likely to hold an Esbat (gathering). These meetings not only provide consistency but also tap into the peak of lunar power.

- Psychic and intuitive forces are at an optimum. Many Wiccans take the opportunity to work with their preferred method of divination.

- Empower new tools in a stream of moonlight enhancing it with an opal mist, Her glistening touch.

- Cast a spell, release a wish. Magick worked upon full moon night often comes to fruition. This is the phase that bears the best results.

- Women, reawaken your feminine power. Infuse your spirit and dance with the Goddess in celebration.

When working with the full moon, I find that my divination skills are heightened, my psychic awareness is tripled, and the ability to manifest my goals becomes more possible.
—PYTHO, AGE 14, MILAN, ITALY

Each month the full moon allows me to reenergize, attain balance, and find peace within the arms of the Mother Goddess. It reminds me of what it means to be a woman, a priestess.
—ARIAWN, AGE 19, OHIO, USA

Moontime

The energy of the full moon is present the day before, day of, and day after it is technically full. This seventy-two-hour time period is helpful because it provides practitioners with two additional nights for holding a Full Moon ritual. As a reminder, the day after the full moon usually contains a slight amount of waning energies. If you intend on working magick during this time you'll want to take this factor into consideration. Celebrating the full moon the day after won't have a negative impact because rituals rarely require the same cautious timing as spell work.

To keep up to date with the moon cycle, it is a good idea to consult a calendar or almanac. The technologically savvy Wiccan can track lunar movements by visiting astrological websites. However, I recommend Llewellyn's astrological datebooks because they are accurate, well-researched, and multifunctional. These datebooks have the benefit of viewing the current moon phase at a glance and can also be used daily for homework notes and appointments.

❧ From Gwinevere's Book of Shadows

October 9, 2001—Age 17

I had a fantastic dream last night. I dreamt that I was in a large Victorian house and it was nighttime. As I walked down a hallway a white light came through a window, flooding the carpet. I slowly approached the light shimmering on the floor; then I looked out the window and saw the fullest moon in a nighttime sky. I was standing in the white blanket of light engulfed head to toe, and the moon smiled down.

The full moon is a very spiritual time. We seek to honor the Goddess and thank Her for our blessings.
—ANUBIS RAINHAWK, AGE 15, CALIFORNIA, USA

Connect with the Lunar Power

To complement ceremony and celebration, practitioners can further attune to the full moon energy by partaking in practices like meditation, journaling, taking nighttime strolls, or creating art. Connecting with lunar power (Goddess energy) allows us to draw upon Her positive vibrations and incorporate them into our life, eventually becoming happier and more balanced. In this section we'll take a look at several small yet meaningful ways to honor and attune to feminine lunar power.

> *Somehow I can feel a connection between me and the moon, like there is a silver string holding us together.*
> —LUNA, AGE 16, FINLAND

MEDITATION

Below you'll find a guided full moon meditation. The goal is to become calm, centered, and connected to lunar energies. You may want to record yourself reading the passage then play the tape back to partake in the exercise, or read it over a few times to get a feel for the imagery and direction. You don't have to memorize every detail but it is important to slowly progress into the meditation and come out of it in a similar fashion.

Find a quiet place where you won't be disturbed, and position yourself comfortably. Close your eyes and let any pent-up negativity drain out of your body and dissipate into thin air. Focus on your breathing: inhale through your nose and exhale through your mouth.

Picture yourself at night standing in a forest, surrounded by trees. As you look at your hands you see them illuminated with light from above. The moon is round and bright. Her rays fill the darkened forest but seem to point to a dirt path in front of you, traveling north. Protected in her safe, luminous light you walk the path and see a clearing beyond the forest. When you approach the clearing, a familiar sound tickles your ear: ocean waves.

The forest is behind you now as you stand barefoot in the sand. The moon is smiling in the clear sky above calm water. You are one with the earth and one with the Goddess. Be still. Open your spirit to her messages. Wait. After a few moments, turn back to the forest, follow the dirt path into the woods, and concentrate on your breathing. Inhale through your nose, exhale through your mouth. Slowly open your eyes and adjust to your surroundings.

Marking the full moon with ritual is a rewarding experience that brings a lot to the surface. It is a time of introspection and meditation, a period where the world's chaos and troubles are momentarily suspended and we may look freely into the mirror of the night sky and truly see who we are.
—GEDE, AGE 15, QUEENSLAND, AUSTRALIA

JOURNALING

I've always believed that taking a few moments to journal or write in a Book of Shadows can benefit the spirit, heart, and mind. Reflecting on divinity in her feminine aspect through journaling can serve yet another purpose—further building a connection with the Goddess. We know the impact of spoken words during magick practice; written ones filled with sacred thoughts, concepts, and ideas also release personal power.

Annotating your spiritual experiences, sharing deep inner yearnings, and expressing tender thoughts of the Goddess can open your soul to the divine. The full moon is an especially good time to partake in this experience because Her energy is potent and readily available for us to draw upon.

The full moon stirs something within me that I believe is an ancient line coursing through the past, present, and future, merging

*the worlds so that I may feel and sense what has come before me,
where I am now, and what lies ahead.*
—GEDE, AGE 15, QUEENSLAND, AUSTRALIA

ADORN HER SYMBOLS

Named after the moon because of its glowing resemblances and
iridescent nature, semiprecious moonstone has feminine energy and is linked to the element of water. Its main associations—protection, love, and psychic abilities are also attributed
to its planetary ruler, the moon. Although moonstone is the
primary lunar symbol, other gemstones/crystals ruled by the
moon include aquamarine, beryl, white chalcedony, clear
quartz crystal, mother-of-pearl, pearl, sapphire, and selenite.

Silver, which is also ruled by the moon, is often used with
feminine gemstones to form necklaces, earrings, bracelets, and
charms. Silver's element is water and has magical properties
similar to that of moonstone. Together or apart, silver and
moonstone are closely connected with the energies of the full
moon and can be worn by practitioners—both male and female—for lunar attunement.

✤ From Gwinevere's Book of Shadows

April 25, 2003—Age 19

While working with moonstone in my jewelry-making, I've become fascinated with this stone! I am in awe that Mother Earth could produce
such a unique semiprecious gem. Hold the piece one way and it looks
white; turn it slightly and glimmers of light blue pop out. I've even come
across pieces that appear to have pink undertones. I definitely understand
why some people have a special affinity for moonstone.

A Nighttime Stroll Under the Full Moon

In my book *Moonbeams & Shooting Stars,* I wrote about an experience I had while walking outside one night. "I looked up and saw the moon gazing down. I remember thinking, what exactly is it about the moon that intrigues me? I don't believe I'll even fully know the answer to that question, but I do have a few guesses. It's milky white, softly beautiful, and simply breathtaking. It follows me wherever I go, as if urging me in the right direction."

Taking a nighttime stroll, if your neighborhood is safe, can turn into a spiritual adventure. Grab a friend or family member, flashlight, and keys and head outside. On a crisp, cool night look to the moon above (the ultimate symbol of our lunar deity) and open your spirit to Her comforting vibrations. Speak this incantation or create your own blessing on the spot.

Moon up above shinning big and bright,
bless me with your silken rays,
upon this luminous night.

Whenever you are bored indoors, add in this ritual to mix up your routine. You'll instantly feel energized and empowered!

Full moon celebrations are very sacred to me because it is easier to communicate with the Goddess. When I go outside and stand under the full moon, it's as if I can feel Her all around me. Her sweet voice speaks to me and I know I'm on the right path.
—Anubis RainHawk, age 15, California, USA

Creative Art

Around the time of the full moon I find that my intuitive, psychic, and creative abilities are enhanced. If you also feel a surge in creativity it's a great idea to funnel and transform that energy into artistic expression. Use that expression to further enhance your link to the Goddess. Create lunar drawings, paintings, collages, or write moon-focused poetry. You can even place your handmade Goddess art on the altar as an offering or deity representation. Become a poet, make an artistic treasure; the full moon is a wonderful time to release your pent-up creativity.

> *The full moon is a time for harvesting, be it ideas, memories, works of art, or feelings, it's time to bring them together. The full moon is whole, ripe, and ready for the picking.*
> —LYNX SONG, AGE 15, LOUISIANA, USA

"Moon Spirit"
by Gwinevere Rain
August 15, 2004

> *Upon this tender night I hear cascading gilmmersong*
> *Kisses if silver light from fairy and fawn*
> *Lunar wishes with glittered hope flutter to the sky*
> *and my moon spirit soars—chasing them up high.*

Full Moon—Blessed Water

Full Moon—blessed water is a combination of the Goddess's lunar power, a practitioner's intent, jar of water, and salt. It is an effective consecration tool with a multitude of uses and plenty of benefits. One to two drops can bless new ritual equipment, empower magical objects, or be used to anoint oneself as a pre-ritual purification. Full Moon—blessed water is an inexpensive, make-it-yourself implement that is a great addition to any Wiccan's magickal stock.

Supplies
Stick of incense
Jar of water (a bowl can be substituted)
Three pinches salt
Piece of paper
Black pen

Perform this ritual on the night of the full moon. If you'd like, cast a protective circle before starting. Bring the supplies to your altar, light the incense stick, and find a comfortable sitting position. Place the jar of water in front of you and keep the salt nearby.

To begin, hold your hand (with open palm facing down) above the water and close your eyes. Visualize a white light or mist coming from your palm, infusing the jar and its contents with positive vibrations. Repeat this visualization while holding your hand above the salt.

Next, take your sheet of paper and draw a pentacle in

the center. Proceed to place the jar on top of the pentacle image and carefully sprinkle three pinches of salt into the water. Through visualization, conjure up a mental image of the full moon. Feel the Goddess energy in your heart and mind.

While moving your hand above the jar in a clockwise motion (as if you are stirring the air) speak this incantation:

"O' Beautiful Goddess, Queen of the night
please send down your silken light
and bless this open vessel filled to brim
along with the liquid contained herein."

Lastly, throw your hands up to the sky and say,
"As I will,
so mote it be."

Your Full Moon—blessed water has been made. Use it for any external purification or empowerment. Keep on your altar to utilize throughout the month. For each full moon, drain the old water and make a fresh batch!

Create a Full Moon Ritual

When a practitioner seeks to honor the Goddess during the full moon he or she is reaching out to the divine with open arms. This beautiful act is best achieved through a personal and private ritual. Using someone else's format lacks emotional depth and personal touch.

The combination of your words and methods worked up on a full moon night shows meaningful expression and reverence. The following set of guided activities will enable you to achieve a personalized ritual that in turn can become a monthly tradition to honor the lunar Goddess.

> *It has only been recently that I have truly appreciated the energy and peace exuded by the full moon and therefore have begun to celebrate more regularly the occasion with ritual.*
> —GEDE, AGE 15, QUEENSLAND, AUSTRALIA

FULL MOON CORRESPONDENCES

Colors: White, silver, light or dark blue, purple (for psychic awareness).

Miscellaneous Symbols: Chalice, cauldron, silver objects, dimes/coins, mirrors, crescent shapes, moon charms, silver bell, Full Moon–blessed water, white, silver, or blue ribbons, glitter or sequins.

Crystals/Gems: Aquamarine, beryl, clear quartz crystal, moonstone, mother-of-pearl, pearl, sapphire, selenite, white chalcedony.

Herbs: Aloe, lemon balm, camphor, coconut, eucalyptus, lemon rind, mints, moonwort, myrrh, sandalwood, willow, wintergreen.

Open/Bloomed Flowers: White Roses, white carnations, gardenia, jasmine, lotus, lily, mallow, magnolia, any white-petaled flowers.

Oils: Lemon essential, sandalwood essential, vanilla fragrance, ylang-ylang essential, jasmine fragrance.

Incense: Jasmine, rose, coconut, lotus, sandalwood.

Drink: Water, lemonade, fruit juice, milk.

Food: Sugar cookies, crescent-shaped bakery goods, marshmallows, vanilla wafers, white meringue cookies, MoonPies, lemon cookie bars, coconut macaroons, vanilla yogurt, papaya, fresh melon.

PREPARATIONS

When marking the full moon with ritual there are several optional preparations you can incorporate for effect and atmosphere. To enhance your altar, utilize a shimmery white cloth, institute a dramatically different arrangement, or add lunar decorations (see correspondence list above for suggestions and ideas).

Pay special attention to clothing and accessories. Consider wearing a flowing robe, cape, or dress to reflect the night's celestial theme. Moon-oriented jewelry, lunar symbols, moonstone, or sterling silver can be worn to connect with Goddess vibrations. Or select foods that correspond to the occasion for the ritual feast (grounding) afterwards.

In your Book of Shadows make notes for any Full Moon ritual preparations that you intend on implementing.

INVOCATIONS

Deity invocations for a Full Moon ritual should reflect the event. Traditionally, the focus is on the Goddess in her "Mother" phase as she beams with love, compassion, and hope. Optimally, practitioners want to invoke the Goddess through Her lunar aspect.

Along with an affirming petition, seeking her presence in sacred space, you'll want to conjure up a proper mental image. How would you like to envision the moon Goddess? As a woman figure adorned in a silken white dress with flowing hair? Or the full moon smiling in open sky with rays of light cascading down? Perhaps you have a special image in mind already.

During this time the God is also invoked and welcomed into sacred space. Use His relationship with the Goddess to weave His part into the ritual. He is the lover and consort, lord of shining stars.

Utilize your Book of Shadows to write your invocations and predetermine a moon goddess visualization. If you're in a rush or running low on creative inspiration, select invocations presented in chapter Three.

RITUAL FOCUS
The time following deity invocations is optimal for making Full Moon–blessed water. The mixture can then be used for purposes of anointing (wrists and third eye) or consecrating special tools used during the main ceremony.

The steps in the main ritual are similar to magick. State your intention, make a physical gesture, and conjure up a mental image. In most Full Moon rituals a flowing poem is written beforehand and read within sacred space. This poetic statement doesn't have to be perfect, but it should come from the heart. Review my poem as an example. Consult the following sources as rough guidelines:

> Wicca: A Guide for the Solitary Practitioner, Scott Cunningham (pp. 124–126)
> The Sacred Round: A Witch's Guide to Magical Practice, Elen Hawke (pp. 97–100)
> The Witch's Master Grimoire, Lady Sabrina (pp. 68 and 69)

Your moon poem can be long or short but ultimately it should reflect the main purpose—honoring the Goddess. Physical

Food for Full Moon Ritual.

gestures can be made before, during, or after the poem is read. Perhaps you can play an instrument (such as a ritual drum), dance, light a candle consecrated with Full Moon–blessed water, or sprinkle white flower petals on your altar. Visualization is incorporated during the action. Many choose to visualize a white mist, Goddess image, or picture the full moon passing between translucent clouds in the night.

In the following journal space, decide if and when you'll make Full Moon–blessed water, write down ideas on ritual gestures, and visualization. Enclose a full moon poem that you've personally written.

Gwinevere's Full Moon Ritual Poem

With howl of wind, wisp of leaves
under your mystical light
milky white

night's delight
la luna, the moon
Goddess of a thousand names
you who kiss the night's clouds
and whispers secrets to the stars
show me your mysteries
silvery light
nighttime's glimmer gleam
bless me
awaken me
oh la luna, the woman in the moon
whose love is fair and true
moon dust, vanilla musk
snuggle my soul in your warm glowing arms
I'll go to the moonlit garden
where silver roses grow
awaken your heart sings the crow
moonstone, candles flickering light
music, dancing, and chanting
I'll sing to you oh lady fair & true
starry love, chants the white dove
la luna, la luna
awaken me, bless me
show me, guide me true
dark night, bright light
with the howl of the wind
wisp of leaves
under your mystical light
awaken my soul
la luna, la luna
the night owl cries
fullest moon in the darkest skies
and so shall it be

I pray to you under the moon so full
awaken my soul, and bless me so
the candlelight dims down, as do the hymns
and all sleeps.

AFTER RITUAL

Once you've completed a Full Moon ritual you'll have the opportunity to work magick, utilize your preferred method of divination, or reflect on the day's significance via a guided meditation. This is also a great point in which to write in your Book of Shadows and detail your Full Moon experience. Some Wiccans decide to continue the celebration and partake in a ritual feast. Whatever you decided to do with your time, enjoy yourself while tapping into the night's power.

NINE

Gwinevere's Spells

While working magick, I don't create anything supernatural, but I do subtly encounter moments of pure witchiness. Many times, when all the candles have been snuffed, incense quenched, and I am sitting before my altar in the darkness, the scent of smoke lingers and I bask in the beautiful silence. My goal still feels fresh and I have an understanding, a deep knowing that I've done my work. I affirm that along with a positive mind-set and continued perseverance, results will manifest. This kind of experience is the underlying essence of magick; it is something that is best felt and learned on one's own.

In this chapter you'll find my personal spells to help stop gossip, invite love, improve study sessions, and more! Before you jump to cast any magick, I highly suggest working in sacred space (see the beginning of chapter Six for more details on why this is an important step). To decipher timing options, see page 179. Finally, don't underestimate your own creativity. You can write your own one-of-a-kind spells; check out chapter Ten for more details.

> *Though there are rules for magick, Wiccans have the freedom to create change in many ways. We are able to work a variety of spells as long as they adhere to the Wiccan Rede.*
> —ANUBIS RAINHAWK, AGE 15, CALIFORNIA, USA

> *Writing my own spells makes me more familiar with the magick. It also allows me to target my specific needs.*
> —LYNX SONG, AGE 15, LOUISIANA, USA

❧ From Gwinevere's Book of Shadows

June 14, 1999—Age 14

I cast my first spell tonight. I was so nervous, I was shaking. It took me about five minutes till I could call the corners. Since I don't have a wand yet, I used an eyeliner pencil that I quickly snatched off my dresser. A rush of adrenaline came over me; magick suddenly went from something I read about to something I can perform.

Stop Gossip

This spell will aid you in suppressing gossip. It may not halt all lingering rumors, but it's an excellent start. If the gossiper is male, change "her to him," during the incantation. Likewise, if you believe there are several gossipers, you'd then change "her to their" and "she'll to they'll."

Supplies
Piece of cream paper
Black pen
Scissors
Picture of a man's or woman's mouth cut from a magazine
Black ribbon measuring about eight inches in length

Gather your supplies and place them in front of you. For the benefit of time, have the magazine image and black ribbon cut out and ready to use. Dim the lights for ambiance or use candles for soft illumination. Mentally focus on the goal.

Write the following magical incantation on cream paper:

"Crone goddess, Earthen One who is sage and wise
aid me in the task to stop all gossip and lies
here upon thy paper I write her name
and dispel those words that hurt and shame
I wish for peace upon this shadowed day
and know soon she'll receive her karmic pay."

In large bold letters underneath the incantation, pen the name of your suspected gossiper. If you aren't aware of the person yet, just write "he/she who gossips about me," in place of the suspect's name. Read the incantation out loud and then place the mouth photo on top of the paper. Visualize your-self happy and free from being the subject of gossip. Focus on your *own life* being positive instead of the gossiper getting payback.

Next, fold the paper in half, making sure the magazine pic-ture doesn't fall out. Start to roll the paper into a scroll and use the black ribbon as a tie. Once the scroll is complete, the spell is done. Keep the scroll out of sight, such as under your bed or at the bottom of a dresser drawer.

Healing Waters

This is a multipurpose healing spell that can be used for your-self or cast on someone you love. It sends positive healing vibes to the particular person but isn't intended to be a cure-all. If possible, keep his or her photograph visible during the spell casting or use powerful visualization to summon a mental picture.

Supplies
Access to the kitchen or bathroom sink
Candles for extra light
Glass of water
Bergamot or eucalyptus oil
Picture of intended healing patient

Set the ambiance for your spell by dimming the lights and in-corporating several lit candles around the sink for illumination. Fill a tall glass with water and stir in three drops of bergamot or eucalyptus oil. Hold your palms above the glass and visualize a white (or blue) healing mist. Mentally picture that positive energy surrounding the cup and infusing the water. Carefully start to pour the liquid down the drain while saying this chant:

"Oh lord and lady
whose love is divine and pure
I summon your majestic power
as care is needed in darkest hour
heal now __'s body, removing hurt and pain
illness gone washed down the drain."

Take a few moments and meditate on the image of the person you're seeking to help. When you're done extinguish any candles you've lit, clear the area, and record the experience in your Book of Shadows.

Prosperity Powder

This powder can be sprinkled in a purse or wallet, on pictures of items you wish to obtain, rubbed on spell candles, used in poppets, mojos, or around your bedroom to invite prosperous energy into your life!

Supplies
Large mixing bowl
1 tablespoon ginger
1 teaspoon dried mint
½ cup of cornstarch
Clear resealable bag or bottle

In a large mixing bowl combine ginger, mint and cornstarch. Stir while visualizing your goal of increasing prosperity, living comfortably, and buying the items you'd like to own. Most of all, picture yourself happy and content with your financial situation. Your visualization can be as general or specific as you'd like.

Say this incantation as you continue to stir:

"Money, riches flow to me, from here or there
to meet my needs with plenty to spare
method be just
magick be fair
for harm to none I do care
universe bring prosperity my way
wealth of treasures come and stay!"

Next, hold your hands above the bowl with palms facing down and infuse the mixture with magical energy. Envision a white light coming from the earth, up through your body, out of your palms, and into the bowl's contents.

Once you've finished stirring and empowering your mixture, store the contents in a resealable bag or bottle. Affix a label with contents, moon phase, and date. Use your powder whenever and wherever you'd like to build prosperous vibes. Speak the above incantation while applying the powder to a particular item or space.

Study Spell

Use this spell to promote well-focused study sessions.

Supplies
Yellow candle with holder
Lemon juice or scented fragrance oil
½ tablespoon ground coffee
3 pinches dried rosemary

Hold the yellow candle between your palms and visualize a positive white light. Anoint the candle with lemon juice, roll it in the coffee grounds, and place in a sturdy holder. Take three pinches of rosemary and sprinkle around the candle in a clockwise motion while saying:

"Windows to my mind open and expand."

Light the wick and meditate for a few moments on your goal. Don't try to picture a specific grade on a test; instead place your focus on improving mental clarity and concentration during study periods. Next, say this chant three times out loud, speaking into the candle flame:

"Seek and bestow
memory grow
lemon scent, coffee brew
In the light, refreshed and new."

When you're ready, extinguish the candle in a manner you feel is appropriate.

Bring the candle to all of your study sessions. Make sure you keep the flames away from lingering papers and important study notes so they don't catch on fire. As long as the candle is in your general vicinity when you study, the magick will continue to empower your goal.

Witchy-Witch Sleep Well Spell

To promote a good night's sleep. Use if there is an important event the following day and you need to be fully rested and attentive. Thi is also a perfect solution to stop nightmares when you're not in a waning moon phase.

Supplies
Muslin mojo pouch
Equal parts chamomile and rosemary herbs

Combine herbs in your muslin bag. Visualize yourself waking up the next morning feeling fantastic! Say the following chant three times as you continue to visualize your desire:

"Upon this night
I caste a witches spell
to prevent nightmares where I dwell
a pinch of chamomile
a dash of rosemary too
so every morning here after
I'll awake refreshed and new!"

Securely close the pouch and inhale its fresh scent. Keep the mojo bag near your bed and inhale the scented pouch before you go to bed each night. Refresh herbs and spell every three months.

Simple Protection Spell

It's not every day you run into a pack of mugwort herb, so here is a quick and simple spell any teen can use when in need of a little protection and comfort.

Supplies
Piece of unlined, blank white paper
Black pen
1 tablespoon salt
1 teaspoon pepper
White envelope

On the blank piece of paper write your name in the center and under that the phrase:

"Protect me in day, in night and all times of fright."

Slowly circle the phrase as you repeat it three times out loud. Next, sprinkle salt and pepper in a circular clockwise motion over the center of the paper. When you're done, say this incantation:

"In the circle, salt n' pepper mound,
protect me well from sky to ground."

Then carefully fold up the paper, making sure the salt and pepper remain inside. Inscribe a large pentacle on the outside along with your craft name. Place the folded paper in a white envelope and seal tight. Keep in a dresser drawer or bury it outside by your bedroom window for protection. Repeat spell whenever you feel it is necessary.

Spell for Inner Peace

Use this spell to help attain inner peace and calm your mind. It is also a wonderful stress-reducer!

Supplies
Small bowl or jar
15 drops grapeseed base oil
5 drops ylang-ylang essential oil
CD of soft meditation music
White candle and holder
Pen
Book of Shadows (or journal)

In the small bowl or jar, combine fifteen drops grapeseed oil and five drops ylang-ylang oil. Mix well and set aside. Dim the lights, turn on your CD, and bring the rest of your supplies to your altar.

Adorn the white candle with your oil mixture and use visualization to rid it of any negative energies. Take a moment to hear the music in the background, and light the candle's wick. Feel the stress leaving your body as you see the wick ignite.

Next, say the following incantation as you gently dab the ylang-ylang oil blend on your wrists and third eye.

"Peace is a flower, white and tranquil
Shining bright in a luminous light

Bloom with hope in my time of need
Sustain balance with this mental seed
Any wrongs in my life turn to rights
By the power of earth, moon, and celestial flights."

Attune yourself with the energy of your favorite Goddess. Lunar deities work especially well with this ritual of inner peace. Meditate on calming thoughts while listening to the soft, soothing music. Write in your Book of Shadows or personal journal, conveying any emotional pain you've felt recently. Expressing your feelings is the best way to release inner fears and conjure up a more positive future.

Success Spell

Use this spell to promote success in all areas of your life. You may want to customize it to focus on a particular area such as school, work ventures, or wealth.

Supplies
White candle with holder
Full Moon–blessed water (see recipe, p. 150)
Silver ribbon cut to 8 inches in length

Hold the candle between your palms and visualize a white mist. Let the positive energy flow around and inside your hands. When you're done with the visualization, proceed to anoint your candle with Full Moon–blessed water. Next, place the candle down on a flat surface and tie the silver ribbon around its base. Create a bow and cut off the excess length.

Take a few moments to mentally conjure up your goal. What kind of success are you seeking? Do you have a particular area in mind? When your thoughts are focused, carefully place the candle in its holder and light the wick while saying this incantation:

"Candle white burning bright
to summon forth the power
silver ribbon tied tight
to weave my future hour
words spoken well with meaning
between time, both awake and dreaming
earth, air, water, and fire
success is my deepest need and desire."

Continue to sit before your candle and mediate on your goal. When you're finished, conclude the spell by saying:

"With harm to none my will be done
so mote it be!"

Blow out or snuff the candle; relight when you need to reaffirm your goal of success.

Protection Mojo

This advanced spell will help you invoke a protection shield and create an herb-filled magical pouch called a mojo bag.

Supplies
1 sandalwood-, frankincense-, or myrrh-scented incense stick
Piece of cream-colored paper
Black pen
12-inch square dark green fabric

At least two of the following herbs for protection: basil, sage, rosemary

Small protection charm such as: a pentacle drawn on a piece of paper; clear quartz crystal; good-luck penny; something personal you associate with protection

8-inch-long piece green ribbon

Gather your ingredients before you. Light the incense stick and stand before your altar or workspace.

Think of the earth and visualize that energy coming through your feet, up your body. Let Mother Earth's energy seep into your limbs, chest, and head. After your visualization is finished, take a seat and place the cream paper in front of you. With the black pen, inscribe your name on the paper and fold into a small square. Put it aside for a few moments.

Lay out the green cloth and sprinkle the herbs directly in its center. Drop your charm and folded paper on top of the herbs. Now, place your hands over this pile and visualize a strong white mist surrounding your body as well as the green cloth and its contents. Feel deity's energy encompassing you, protecting your entire body, mind, and soul. When you're ready, speak these words with meaning and power:

"Incense, herbs and charm
combine and shield against harm
by this protection aura I create
nothing bane shall enter or penetrate."

Feel your shield of protection surrounding you. Pull the edges of the green cloth up into the center (making sure all of the spell ingredients stay inside the cloth) and use the ribbon to tie a knot around the middle. Complete the spell and seal its energy by saying:

*"Magick bind invisibly
as I will, so mote it be."*

Leave the mojo on your altar for the night, then store it in a safe place, like a dresser drawer or nightstand. Visualize your protection shield whenever you need a boost of Goddess comfort.

Love Invitation

The items used in this spell will help you summon romantic love. You'll be asked to create an invitation outlining the traits you'd like to have in a significant other.

Supplies
Apple juice or a sweet drink
Piece of white paper
Red pen
Pinch ground cinnamon
Red envelope

Pour your special drink in a beautiful cup before you begin and bring it to your working area; set it out of the way so you don't accidentally knock it over. Then, place the white paper flat out in front of you and close your eyes. Think about all the inner qualities you desire in a partner; e.g., honest, caring, thoughtful. When you have a detailed mental list, use the top half of the paper to jot it down.

Afterward, softly read those ideals out loud and then take a sip of your drink. Proceed to write down the physical attributes you wish the person to have. Be as detailed as you'd like. Again, speak those desires out loud and then take another sip of your drink.

Once you feel both lists have been completed, hold one hand over the paper and say this incantation:

*"I list this list for all that you are
I call to you be near, naught far."*

Continue by writing the following poem directly in the center of the sheet.

*On this paper, I do invite
my intentions just and right
sprinkled once cinnamon spice
for your kisses I crave, soft and nice
come to me with an open heart
woven magick begin and start!*

Now, draw a heart around the poem and sign your name at the bottom. Take a pinch of cinnamon and sprinkle it over the invitation. Carefully fold the invite, making sure the spice doesn't fall out. To complete the spell, place the paper inside your red envelope and write the words "harm none" on the front. Seal and keep in a special place.

Employment Spell

This spell has been created to help attract the right job for you at this time. You'll find the best results if it is used in conjunction with ordinary means and a strong effort during a job search.

Supplies
2 sheets of white or green tissue paper cut into 10 x 10"
    squares
3 nickels
1 teaspoon cinnamon
1 teaspoon mint
Small piece lemon or lime citrus rind

To begin, gather your ingredients and set them on your altar. Lay the tissue papers out flat on top of one another. Hold the nickels in one hand and using your free hand, sprinkle both herbs in the center of the paper. Drop the citrus rind on top of the mound and hold your palm facedown over the mixture. Say the following invocation:

"Employment is what I seek to find,
by cinnamon, mint, and citrus rind
coins of silver at new moon
Goddess, help this magick boon
come forth now, what's destined for me
As I will, so mote it be!"

Making sure the herbs stay in the center, proceed to fold the tissue into a small pouch. Place the coins on top and leave overnight. In the morning, take the nickels off the magick pouch. Give one coin away when purchasing something, keep another in your wallet or purse, and leave the third on your altar. Bury the magick pouch as soon as possible, sending your request into Mother Earth.

Nixing Bullies

The purpose of this spell is to help you regain control of your life and stop a destructive person's influence.

Supplies
1 frankincense- or sandalwood-scented incense stick
Piece of paper
Red pen
1 teaspoon each of at least two of the following herbs: basil, pine needles, rosemary, or garlic powder
Black marker
Cup of steaming hot water
1 teaspoon of salt
Small shovel or garden tool for digging

Find a quiet place to work and gather all of your supplies except the water and salt. Carefully ignite the incense and inhale the fresh scent. Lay out the blank piece of paper and think about the person who is upsetting your life. With the red pen, inscribe the words *My Bully* at the top. Speak this incantation in a firm voice:

"Heed this witches warning
stop your evil ways and leave me be

you have no power over me
I cast your negative influence out
and leave no room for fear or doubt."

Close your eyes and visualize a white mist surrounding yourself in protection. When you're done, open your eyes to write the following poem in the center of your spell paper:

As darkness is to night
and light is to day
I prevent you from harming me in any way.

Sprinkle your herbs in the center while visualizing yourself happy, peaceful, and safe. Fold the sheet of paper, making sure the herbs are tucked safely inside. Using the black marker, draw a large pentacle on each side of the folded herb packet.

Extinguish any candles and incense in the area and close up your circle if you choose to cast one or cut a doorway to leave. Bring your herbal packet with you. In the cup of hot water, carefully sprinkle 1 teaspoon salt and mix well. Make your way outside and find an out-of-the-way spot in your yard. Dig a hole with your tool, drop in the spell packet, and reflect for a moment on the situation. Realize that you are taking back your power. Slowly pour the hot water over the herbal packet in the dirt and say this spoken charm:

"To mother earth I send,
problem fix and mend."

Cover the hole back up with dirt and stomp on the mound three times. Turn around and walk away. It is done.

TEN

Magick Happens!

Wiccans work positive magick to help ourselves and aid loved ones. We align with universal energy to create, alter, mold, shape, and improve. Once a combination of circumstances—deep desire, firm intent, corresponding supplies, a well-written personalized spell, protective circle, diving blessing and excellent timing—are brought into harmony, magick happens and change is set into motion. Magick is a beautiful tool of personal empowerment and transformation that should be respected and honored.

The bulk of this chapter deals with external elements of magick, but there are also internal aspects that contribute to the spellcraft process. First is the desire. Each magical goal initially comes from the practitioner; whether it is a desire to help another or oneself, it is the catalyst that starts a particular spell. Placing careful thought and deliberation into the future work is a natural follow-up. This chain of events is detailed in chapter Two under magickal ethics.

Focus on the desire before and during the spell-casting process. Without the ability to concentrate, visualize, and consistently push forth, magick often gets put off or set aside. Keep focused to drive magick from start to completion.

The practitioner's heart should be strongly affected by the magickal goal. Our emotions connect to the need and are felt while reciting an incantation or chanting a special phrase. After the magick has been cast, your belief in the spell sends subtle nudges, influencing the end result. Have faith in yourself and your inner power to create change. Lastly, persistence is a necessity. Sometimes, a complex goal may require more than one attempt. Each try builds energy, but give the goal time to work. Stay strong and positive.

Utilize the correspondences in this chapter along with the Spell Plan on page 199 to create your own bewitching spells!

Most important to the advancement of magickal practice is the use of meditation to learn how to focus and shift consciousness. Clearing your mind, visualizing a single object for as long as possible, doing pathwork—all of these and similar practices help us to learn how to focus.
—ARIAWN, AGE 19, OHIO, USA

When I first started practicing magick, I was all about the spells. Now I am learning more about the nature of magick.
—LYNX SONG, AGE 15, LOUISIANA, USA

❧ From Gwinevere's Book of Shadows

March 27, 2003—Age 19

I had a weird feeling of negativity, which came from a nightmare that haunted me throughout the day. I decided something needed to be done. Once the house was quiet, I took advantage of the time and privacy. A storm was just coming in off the coast. My energy was high and I was in good spirits. I sat on my bed, focused on my goal, and wrote up a special chant. It didn't come out perfect right away, it took some time. A dash of editing. I gathered my incense: one stick of patchouli, another of sandalwood, and carefully lit them. I read the chant for the first time, my heart started to beat fast.

I was home alone so I knew I could use a loud voice if I had wanted. Normally my spells are whispered, so the impact of a loud, full tone almost took me by surprise. I instinctually knew to continue, so I kept reading out loud, line by line. My confidence grew; no longer did my voice sound small. The witch in me took over. I was tracing the perimeter of my room, purifying the space. I repeated the chant so many times, I lost count.

The thunder rumbled softly as if aching, moaning. I felt it travel beneath my feet. Finally, I stood in front of my altar, looked down toward my glowing candles, and stopped the chant. My heart slowed and the words *so mote it be* came to mind. I spoke them once and it was enough. I smiled, blew out my candles, smudged the incense, and made some lunch.

Magical Timing

To obtain the desired result of a particular spell, practitioners pay attention to when it will be cast and what influences are involved. Magical timing doesn't have to be complicated, overwhelming, or intensely detailed. It can be as simple as you'd like, such as casting a spell for improving self-love during the waxing moon.

For more advanced magical timing, take the spell and cast it during the gaining moon, but also incorporate the day of the week that best relates to the intent. In this case, Friday is optimal because it is ruled by Venus, the planet named after the Roman goddess of love. Monday is a great alternative because it is ruled by the moon that oversees matters of emotional healing. In this section we'll address different aspects of magical timing from the basic lunar cycle to daily planetary influences and seasonal transitions.

MOON PHASES

The moon cycle is one of the rhythmic heartbeats of nature. Many practitioners align themselves with the energy of the different phases to cultivate goals and empower magick. Before casting a spell, he or she picks the lunar period that effectively suits their desired outcome. In this section, we'll go over the vibrations present during each phase and discuss how to harness that power.

The approximate twenty-eight-day cycle commences when the moon is mostly shaded and the smallest crescent is visible. This is the new moon, and releases fresh energy. It is a time to start new projects, plan for the future, contemplate important goals, purify, bless, and consecrate. Over several nights the moon subtly appears to increase. The waxing phase enables us to multiply, build, grow, draw in, and expand. Once the moon reaches its entirety and fullness, magick is at its peak. Work spells for important tasks that require sustained results. The full moon marks a time of positive change and transition. Over the course of several evenings, the moon appears to decrease. This waning period carries vibrations associated with letting go, minimizing, stopping negativity, and banishing destructive influences.

Lastly, the Dark of the Moon (or simply Dark Moon) completes the lunar cycle. This phase isn't necessarily scientific, but it is used in Wicca to define the aspect of the moon when no crescent is visible and the moon is completely shadowed. Occurring one or two nights before the new moon, the Dark of the Moon is a time of endings and deep reflection. Magically banishing, binding, shielding, and other defensive magick is undertaken. Check an astrological almanac, calendar, or datebook to learn the precise day in which the moon is new or full.

DAILY MAGICAL INFLUENCES

Each day of the week has a ruling planet or celestial body. Their energy impacts the magical associations of that particular day. Combine the best moon phase and day that suits your spell, or utilize the days of the week on their own. Experiment and decide which method works for you!

Sunday
Ruled by: Sun   Gender: Masculine
Success, prosperity, courage, strength, leadership, power, protection, healing, spirituality.

Monday
Ruled by: Moon   Gender: Feminine
Psychic awareness, intuition, sleep, peace, prophetic dreams, divination, fertility, compassion, healing (especially emotions).

Tuesday
Ruled by: Mars   Gender: Masculine
Passion, action, change, overcoming problems, courage, strength, protection.

Wednesday
Ruled by: Mercury   Gender: Masculine
Communication, travel, learning, studying, wisdom, divination.

Thursday
Ruled by: Jupiter   Gender: Masculine
Prosperity, abundance, money, growth, business, jobs, luck, legal issues.

Friday
Ruled by: Venus   Gender: Feminine
Love, beauty, youth, harmony, joy, friendships, fidelity in relationships.

Saturday
Ruled by: Saturn   Gender: Feminine
Defense magick, banishing, binding, shielding, endings, homes and houses.

SEASONS AND MAGICK

Spring *(March, April, May)*
Beginnings, new projects, purification, cleansing, planting a magical garden (herbs and flowers grown with the purpose of using them in future magical workings), fertility, finding love, beauty, partnerships, happiness.

Summer *(June, July, August)*
Money, prosperity, success, goals, strength, courage, fire magick, keeping love strong, fidelity, physical healing.

Fall *(September, October, November)*
Spirituality, giving thanks for blessings, banishing negativity, protection, new possessions.

Winter *(December, January, February)*
Reflecting inward, meditation, emotional healing, divination, psychic awareness, seeking past lives.

MAGICAL COLORS

Colors play a special role in magick. Each shade gives off its own type of energy. For example, when you see a pastel pink flower, it appears soft and subtle. On the other hand, orange can appear bright and release a feeling of vibrancy. When creating a spell, many practitioners decide upon a color, its energy, and corresponding connection to the overall intent. We consider colors when selecting a cord (or ribbon) for knot magick, fabric color to create mojo bags or poppets, and especially the shade of wax for candle magick.

Bringing color into the spell process establishes a visual link to the goal. Since colors may mean different things to different people, I'd like you to come up with your own set of correspondences. Review the list below and jot down in your Book of Shadows which color you feel would best match each goal. Don't worry about being "wrong." You can always change your answers later. If you're stuck, consult a Wiccan book or website that lists color correspondences and see if you agree or disagree with the provided material.

Banishing	Money	Purification
Beauty	Peace	Sleep
Desire	Protection	Success
Healing	Psychic Aware-	Wishes
Love	ness	

TYPES OF MAGICK

In this section we'll take a look at several types of magick used by Wiccans. By no means is this a complete list; there are other aspects of spellcraft that practitioners also perform. Additionally, please consider this information a rough guideline. Alter, add, or subtract any steps in the suggested format. Wiccan magick isn't meant to be kept in a forced structure. Follow your intuition and have fun creating your own personalized spells!

> *By learning different systems of magick I am able to utilize my knowledge from all practices and form my own unique blend.*
> —PYTHO, AGE 14, MILAN, ITALY

> *Fire magick, which incorporates candles is my forte. I am also comfortable using conjuring bags and knot magick.*
> —GEDE, AGE 15, QUEENSLAND, AUSTRALIA

Candle Magick

Select a candle with a corresponding color to represent your goal (see color information in this chapter). It is important that you also have a secure holder that works with your candle's size and shape. To begin, consecrate the candle in a way that you feel is most appropriate. This may include visualization, passing it through incense smoke, sprinkling the base with Full Moon–blessed water, or utilizing an alternative method.

The next step is referred to as "dressing" the candle. There are various ways to go about this. One concept is to rub an oil (that also matches the magickal desire) around the base in a clockwise motion. At your discretion, this action can be accompanied by visualization and reciting an incantation. Additionally, carving a symbol on the side of the candle or rolling it in herbs may also follow.

After the candle has been dressed it is placed in the holder and the wick is lit. While visualizing the final outcome, chant a magical phrase or read an incantation to clearly state your goal. Often, I write my desire on a sheet of paper, roll it up into a scroll, tie it with a ribbon, and keep near the spell candle to affirm my desire. Finally, the candle is extinguished. It can be re-lit on the following night(s) to restate your magical desire and continue to feed energy into the spell.

It is important to note that some practitioners believe blowing out a spell candle disrupts the magick. If you agree, then consider adding a snuffer to your tool collection. In the past I have blown out spell candles purposefully believing that breath can give magick life and release my goal into the universe. Currently, I use a snuffer because it is more efficient. The end result of my magick has not been compromised when utilizing either method. Experiment and see what works best for you!

> *I prefer using candles to many other types of magick. I don't know if it is the energy of the flame or the soothing effect of dancing firelight.*
> —Chiron Nightwolf, age 16, Georgia, USA

Mojo Bag (also called herbal sachet or conjuring bag)
Select herbs that match your goal and place them on your altar or working space. Use a premade fabric bag or cut a square piece of cloth (about six inches in length and width). Consider the fabric color so that it corresponds with your goal or use white, which is all-purpose. Cut a lengthy ribbon or string, again paying attention to color theme so that you'll be able to tie the bag later in the process. Find or make a charm to enhance your connection to the magickal desire. These symbols can be nickels for money; a pentacle drawn on paper for protection; a tiny mirror for beauty; or heart candy for love.

To begin, combine your herbs and place them in the fabric bag (or pile them in the center of your cloth). Add the charm. Hold your hand over the mixture and visualize to empower the ingredients. Recite your chant or incantation. Then close the fabric pouch with one hand and tie it with the ribbon. If you're using a flat piece of cloth, pull the ends up, leaving the mixture in the center and carefully use the ribbon to seal the bag. Hold the final product, inhale the herbs, and visualize your magickal goal.

Knot Magick

Gather satin rattail cord or embroidery floss in a color that corresponds with your magickal desire. Cut it to nine inches, which is the result of the number three (a sacred number to Wiccans) multiplied by itself. Bring the cord along with a pen and a small sheet of paper to your altar or working space. Count the lines in your chant or incantation. Write the number on the corner of your paper. This figure will be used to determine the amount of knots you'll tie during the spell (for example, if there are four lines, you'll be making four knots).

To begin, think about your spell and mentally picture the end result. When you're ready, write on the paper this phrase: "My goal is to ___." Fill in the blank with your magickal desire (e.g., become successful, invite love, release pent-up negativity).

Proceed to pick up the cord and hold the ends taut. Infuse it with your positive vibrations and energy from the divine by visualizing white mist coming from the earth, up your body, and out into the cord. Next, start tying the knots. To increase, build, or invite, start your first knot at the left and move across the cord toward the right. To release, banish, or decrease start at the right and work toward the left. Remember, the number of knots you'll make depends on the number you wrote on the paper during preparation.

After each of your knots have been tied, hold the cord in your hands as you recite the chant or incantation. While visualizing your goal seal the spell by giving the cord a kiss. Leave it on your altar, dresser, carry it with you, or bury it. Don't undo the knots unless you wish to undo the spell.

> *Last year a girl on my floor in college asked me to help her with her communication problems she'd been having with her boyfriend, and so I developed a bit of cord magick. It is almost a year later and they are still together and talking openly.*
> —ARIAWN, AGE 19, OHIO, USA

Poppets

A poppet is a fabric doll shaped like an oversized gingerbread cookie. They are used to bring about positive results, not to curse, hex, or cause harm. Poppets generally require more time and money on supplies than other types of magick, but it is very "hands-on," which in my experience is beneficial to the end result.

This type of sympathetic spellcraft works in a unique way. First, the doll is created to symbolically represent the person who the spell is meant for. Then, it is empowered to bring about a specific magickal goal. The idea is to direct energy by utilizing symbolism, herbs, and visualization. There are three stages to working poppet magick; each plays its own part in the spell process.

Step One: Prepare

It's a good idea to start with a pattern. Do this by taking a sheet of 8½ x 11" printer paper and drawing a large gingerbread figure. Use as much of the paper as possible because the poppet will end up smaller than your pattern. Once you're happy with the shape, cut it out and set it aside. The next preparation task involves selecting material for your doll. Craft stores carry a wide range of fabric. Silky fabrics are difficult to work with. Aim for cotton, preferably in a color that corresponds to your goal. Muslin is a great all-purpose natural fabric that is cost-effective, often under $2 a yard.

While you're at the craft store, check out spools of colored ribbons, and don't forget to grab a medium-sized needle and thread. Keep an eye out for stuffing, as the doll will need to be filled later on. Stuffing options vary; white fluff is common, but cotton balls or white yarn make great substitutions. Decorative faux moss, another stuffing option, can be messy but does the job. Select herbs that correspond with your goal and create a charm (or Taglock) that will be used to symbolically link the person to the poppet. Taglock examples are a handwriting sample, something small that belongs to them, or a picture of the person. Alternatively the doll can represent a situation such as halting gossip. In this case, don't assign the poppet any personal qualities or Taglocks. Instead, write on a piece of paper, "stop gossip" and use that as your charm.

Step Two: Create

To begin, gather your sewing supplies: fabric, pattern, marker, scissors, needle, and thread. Lay the pattern over the fabric and use the marker to carefully trace the pattern on to the material. Repeat this step, in order to create two identical poppet shapes on your fabric. Proceed to cut out the shapes but make sure to cut one centimeter outside of the black line. Lay the poppet shapes on top of each other.

With your needle and thread, start to sew along the edge using the marker line as your guide. At this point, you're molding the shapes together. Important note: For stuffing purposes, you'll want to leave two inches unsewn on one of the legs.

Once you're done sewing the poppet (and left a two-inch hole in its leg) make a firm knot and snip off any remaining thread. Use the hole in the poppet's leg to carefully turn poppet inside out. This step hides most of your stitching and gives a better appearance.

Step Three: Empower

At this point in the process, it is a good idea to work in a sacred space, within your circle or at your altar. Bring the rest of your supples to the working area: poppet, stuffing, Taglock/charm, and herbs. Optional materials include colored ribbons for decoration, and markers or paints to make facial features. Use the hole in the poppet's leg to stuff the doll. As you do this, visualize your goal and the end result you are seeking.

Once you're ready, tuck your herbs into the poppet. Make sure they reach the head and chest area. Now is a great time to decorate the doll: add eyes, nose, and mouth, and tie ribbons around its wrist. Finally, work the Taglock or charm into the midsection of the poppet. Once it's firmly in one spot, hold the doll while visualizing a mist coming from the earth, up your body, out your hands, and into the poppet. Recite your chant or incantation. Stitch the hole in the poppet's leg or use a safety pin to close the opening.

After you've completed the spell, you'll want to find a safe place to keep the doll. Leave on your altar, tuck in a dresser drawer, or keep in an empty shoe box.

HERBS

Working with herbs connects our spirit to the divine because they are a direct product of nature. When I hear the crunch of chamomile in a mojo bag, smell the aroma of eucalyptus stuffed in a healing poppet, or see sage bundles smoldering, it awakens my senses and sparks the magical fire within.

Below I've enclosed the properties of several herbs that may already be in your kitchen cabinet, or can be found locally at many food stores. Although in culinary terms ginger is a root and nutmeg is a spice, for practical purposes, I tend to place spices, roots, nuts, and seeds under the umbrella term *herb*.

Anise Seed—Wards off nightmares, aids in protection, purification.

Basil—Wards off negativity, aids in protection, prosperity, love.

Chamomile—Aids in sleep, purification, attracts money, love.

Cinnamon—Great multipurpose herb that aids in success, desire, love, protection, healing, spirituality. Enhances psychic awareness, increases power.

Eucalyptus—Aids in healing, protection.

Ginger—Aids in success, love, attracts money, and increases magical power.

Marjoram—Great multipurpose herb that aids in love, health, protection. Attracts money, improves happiness.

Mint—Wards off negativity, attracts money, desire. Aids in healing, protecting the home, protection during travel.

Nutmeg—Aids in prosperity, luck, health, fidelity. Enhances psychic awareness, increases magical power.

Parsley—Sacred to the goddess Persephone. Aids in purification, protection, desire.

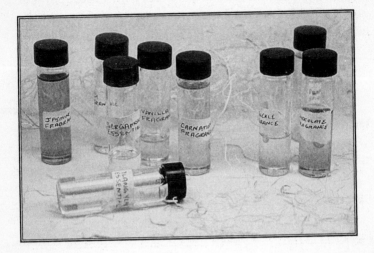

Rosemary—Wards off negativity, aids in purification, clarity, love, desire, healing, sleep.

Sage—Aids in clarity, memory, wisdom, healing, protection, wishes, attracts money.

Thyme—Great multipurpose herb that wards off nightmares, aids in sleep, purification, health, love, enhances psychic awareness, courage.

The following list contains herbs that are harder to acquire but often used in magick. Since you probably won't have them in your kitchen, check metaphysical stores or the Internet.

Dragon's blood—Resin from palm tree that aids in protection, warding off negativity. Combine with other herbs to enhance their magical powers.

Mugwort—Popular witches herb that aids in divination, prophetic dreams, enhancing psychic awareness, astral projection, healing, protection.

Patchouli—Aids in attracting money, prosperity, love, desire, fertility.

Vervain—Great multi-purpose herb that aids in sleep, peace, healing purification, protection, love, money.

Yarrow—Aids in drawing love, friendship, courage, enhances psychic awareness, wards off negativity.

❧ From Gwinevere's Book of Shadows

August 14, 1999—Age 15

I purchased seed packages of lemon balm and rosemary. My plan is to grow the herbs in pots then once they get full and lush, transfer them to the garden. Afterwards, I'll cut them and hang to dry. I want to used my herbs in magick to fill mojo bags, sprinkle around candles, and stuff poppets. The only problem is that, well, I can't seem to grow anything. The fact that I am Wiccan and supposed to be "one with nature" doesn't seem to motivate herbs to cooperate.

CRYSTALS AND GEMSTONES

Amethyst is a beautiful purple stone that varies in hues from light to dark. Its main magical properties center around improving psychic awareness, divination, bringing prophetic dreams, and boosting natural intuition. Amethyst's receptive energy aids the

> ❧ From Gwinevere's Book of Shadows
>
> *September 13, 1999—Age 15*
>
> My attempt at growing herbs was not successful. The rosemary seeds sat there, buried in this big pot of dirt, mocking me, and the lemon balm apparently does not like to be watered twice a day. I realize now with all the water I was feeding it, the poor little seedlings must have felt that Niagra Falls came for a visit. All I have to say now is thank goodness that the food store sells dried culinary herbs in the baking aisle or else I'd have to take up a whole new type of magick!

user in matters of love and happiness. This spiritual stone is linked to the element of water and releases peaceful vibrations.

Aventurine is a beautiful energetic green stone that uplifts the spirit and promotes happiness. This projective stone, ruled by the element of air, also brings good luck and money, sparks creative energy, and boosts feelings of joy. Aventurine is said to speed up healing, improve upon mental powers, and build confidence.

Blue lace agate is a soft blue stone with bands of milky white. It aids in communication, allowing the individual to articulate his or her feelings and ideas. Blue lace agate opens your consciousness to spirit guides, letting important messages come through. It is a feminine water stone, which helps sharpen mental focus and release negative thoughts.

Carnelian is a bright orange stone that promotes a sense of inner harmony. Its projective energy aids in building confidence and helps achieve personal success. Linked to the element of fire, carnelian sparks one's creativity and supports artistic ventures.

Citrine is a translucent warm yellow stone that helps prevent nightmares and supports a restful night's sleep. Associated with the element of fire, this stone helps enhance psychic awareness and sharpen intuition. Citrine's projective energy allows the user to sift through emotional baggage, release self-doubt, and clear the way for happiness.

Hematite is a smooth, silver-colored mineral that promotes inner harmony and calmness. It's a projective stone, used during mediation and healing rituals. Hematite is also said to draw loving energies and aid in long-term commitments. This stone's element is fire, which helps promote deep understanding and aids in spiritual growth. Use hematite to banish negativity and ground you in the present moment.

Iolite is deep violet in color and translucent in nature, and aids in psychic awareness and expansion. This highly spiritual stone will help you feel (inner) unconditional love, and is said to be used by shamans to achieve visions. If used during meditation, iolite will help expand your spiritual growth and understanding of the universe's messages. Associated with the third eye and element of air, it will bring about protection to the individual wearing it.

Moonstone is a milky-white stone most often associated with lunar energies. It is considered to be receptive, improving psychic awareness and intuition. Moonstone's main themes are protection and love. Its feminine water energy aids in peace, tranquillity, emotional healing, and blessings. Moonstone empowers the individual and is prized among witches for its soft, elegant vibrations.

Onyx is an opaque black stone often worn as jewelry. This stone's main magical property is protection. Linked to the ele-

ment of fire and containing projective energy, onyx is used in defensive magick such as banishing or binding spells. The dark color absorbs and cleanses negativity. It is also said to help with clarity of divination.

Peridot is a translucent yellow-green stone that promotes self-love. Its main magical properties include wealth, prosperity, and protection. Peridot's receptive energy helps improve psychic ability, allowing one to see past people's facades. This stone is also used to support good health. Peridot is said to aid in relaxation and restful sleep.

Rose quartz is a translucent pink stone most often used to promote love in all forms. This stone's abilities range from attracting romance, to maintain fidelity, remove loneliness, and instill happiness. Place over your heart to heal emotional wounds. This receptive stone brings peace, friendships, and can give a boost of self-esteem to the wearer. Lastly, rose quartz is said to bring money, banish negativity, and help cleanse your emotions.

❧ From Gwinevere's Book of Shadows

September 10, 2003—Age 19

Herbs, oils, and incense surrounded the space with floral sweet scents. As I held a piece of rose quartz and started visualizing, my hand felt warm. I switched the stone to my other one; it was still warm. It was a soft sensation, not burning, but persistent. I've worked with semi-precious stones for jewelry making and on rare occasions during rituals, but I can honestly say, I've never had this happen before. It wasn't a creepy thing, but certainly the feeling left me perplexed.

MAGICAL WORDS

One of the most important parts of writing a spell is creating a chant or incantation. The magical words provide a venue to detail your exact need. Coming up with them can sometimes feel like a challenge, but ultimately the end result brings a sense of satisfaction.

Why is this aspect of the spell relevant? Because when you verbally express your desire through a chant or incantation, you give it meaning and direction. It is a simultaneous process, you hear the words, feel the magick, and connect with divinity. What is the difference between a chant and incantation? A chant is the repetition of a small phrase multiple times. An incantation is a longer statement that is recited once in a firm voice.

How can you create the magickal words for your spell? Start

with your goal. Write down concepts and ideas that pop into your head when you think of your magical desire. For example, if I am seeking protection, I immediately have the imagery of safe arms embracing me in a hug. I put that into a rhyme creating this;

"O' Goddess and God
embrace me in your light
please keep me safe tonight."

When looking for more unique phrases I consider the supplies that I intend to use during my magick. If I have a new altar to consecrate, I'll probably reach for Full Moon–blessed water. Here is a special incantation I instituted with that in mind:

"By Full Moon water, my personal brew
I cast out negative residue
and banish yucky vibes from this space
to consecrate and bless this magical place."

Wording for a spell sounds best when it rhymes. However, if you can't seem to accomplish this task, state your goal in the form of a clear, concise request.

Sometimes I write my own spells and sometimes I modify some-
one else's spells.
—LUNA, AGE 16, FINLAND

Before writing a spell, I usually meditate on the situation first, so
that I have a clear view on what needs to happen. This helps me
to compose a spell that will have the greatest possible outcome.
—CHIRON NIGHTWOLF, AGE 16, GEORGIA, USA

SPELL-WRITING INCANTATIONS

Every now and then when I am trying to create a new spell, I have a mental block. I feel stuck, as if my thoughts aren't in order or I don't even know where to begin! I created these incantations to promote more productive spell-writing sessions. I encourage you to utilize them whenever you need that extra push in the right direction.

To begin, bring your Book of Shadows and a pen to your altar or sacred space. There is no need to cast a circle but a quick area cleansing with incense or ritual broom won't hurt!

Focus on your spell's intent, the exact goal you want to accomplish. Take a deep breath, close your eyes, and exhale, letting out any frustration or confusion blocking your thought process. Speak this incantation, filling in the blank with your spell's main purpose:

> *"Creativity come to light*
> *for this spell of ___ I intend to write."*

As an alternative use this incantation if you're having difficulties creating the spell's spoken charm:

> *"Form on paper, conjure in mind*
> *send to me the words I seek to find."*

These incantations won't solve all your spell-writing struggles, but hopefully you'll gain a more focused mind frame to get the job done!

Spell Plan

There are eight steps to creating your own spells:

1. Describe the magical goal as well as who the spell is intended to help.

2. Research timing: moon phase, day of the week, etc.

3. Select a color theme that best suits the goal.

4. Decide upon the type of magick you'll use.

5. Make a list of supplies such as herbs, oils, etc.

6. Create a chant or incantation.

7. Predetermine the visualization.

8. Pull each of the above elements together and write out the spell.

I find it helpful to create a quick checklist on a scrap of paper so I can walk around my room, gather the supplies, and mark them off as I go along. Keep track of your spells by photocopying the Ritual and Spell Sheet provided in the back of chapter One. Place in your Book of Shadows and fill in a new line each time you work a ritual or cast a spell.

When I write my own spells, I have already begun to set the spell in motion because I have invested my personal power.
—Anubis RainHawk, age 15, California, USA

Psychic Protection Shield

It is often suggested that practitioners create some method of sacred space, whether it is a formal circle casting or small area cleansing. The main purpose is to protect yourself, your ritual, and the area from negative influences. The following shielding ritual serves a similar purpose: to protect your aura and sensitive psychic mind from further negative energy.

Supplies
Small bottle or jar filled with 3 tablespoons of salt
Medium-size bowl

To begin, sit comfortably before your altar, and place your supplies within arm's reach. Focus your mind on the task. Take three sequential breaths, inhaling deeply through your nose and exhaling slowly out your mouth. While your body is easing into a relaxed state, close your eyes and visualize the area between your eyebrows (also known as the third eye) glowing with a golden light. Softly open your eyes and pick up the small bottle of salt. Hold your left hand over the bowl and sprinkle half the salt over it, allowing the salt to fall off your palm and between your fingers. Dust off lingering salt. Repeat once again but alternate hands (pour with the left onto the right).

Bring up the previously visualized image of your third eye and make the golden light expand around your head and down your body, covering you completely.

Speak the following incantation out loud in a firm voice:

"Maiden, Mother, Crone, Goddess of three
please seal harm away from me
up with light my sacred shield
all negativity turn and yield
as I will, so mote it be!"

To conclude the ritual, toss a pinch of salt over each shoulder and another down in front between your feet. Visualize the psychic protection shield whenever you feel the need to halt negativity from disturbing your aura or from entering your personal space.

Parting Thoughts

riting *Confessions of a Teenage Witch* has been a tremendous journey with months of intense work. During this time period I encountered multiple rewrites (self-inflicted), three hurricanes (all Mother Nature), learning to drive (with my mother bracing herself), peculiar anxiety the week of my twentieth birthday (I survived), and finding the cure for writer's block (chocolate).

During this creation process I have realized how much I've grown in my practice. Reviewing the many pages of my Book of Shadows collection revealed a passion for Wicca, an eagerness to learn, and a continuous craving for positive change.

I have also come to see how insightful the teen contributors are with their individual practices. It is truly unique to be able to open oneself up and express personal experiences to aid others on a beautiful path.

Finally, it is my sincere hope that you, the reader, have attained not only a better understanding from this guide, but also further ways to expand your physical and spiritual practice. May the Goddess and God watch over you with love.

Blessed Be,
Gwinevere Rain

Bibliography

Conway, D.J. *Lord of Light & Shadow: The Many Faces of the God.* St. Paul, MN: Llewellyn, 1997.

Cunningham, Scott. *Cunningham's Encyclopedia of Crystal, Gem, and Metal Magic.* St. Paul, MN: Llewellyn, 1997.

Cunningham, Scott. *Cunningham's Encyclopedia of Magical Herbs.* St. Paul, MN: Llewellyn, 2002.

Cunningham, Scott. *Living Wicca: A Further Guide for the Solitary Practitioner.* St. Paul, MN: Llewellyn, 2000.

Cunningham, Scott. *Wicca: A Guide for the Solitary Practitioner.* St. Paul, MN: Llewellyn, 1999.

Dubats, Sally. *Natural Magick: The Essential Witch's Grimoire.* New York: Kensington Publishing Corp., 2002.

Duff, Gail. *Seasons of the Witch: Celebrating the 8 Wiccan Festivals of the Year.* Berkeley, CA: Ulysses Press, 2003.

Hawke, Elen. *In the Circle: Crafting the Witches' Path.* St. Paul, MN: Llewellyn, 2001.

Hawke, Elen. *Sacred Round: A Witch's Guide to Magical Practice.* St. Paul, MN: Llewellyn, 2002.

McCoy, Edain. *Magick & Rituals of the Moon.* St. Paul, MN: Llewellyn, 2001.

McCoy, Edain. *The Sabbats: A New Approach to Living the Old Ways.* St. Paul, MN: Llewellyn, 2002.

Monaghan, Patricia. *The New Book of Goddesses and Heroines.* St. Paul, MN: Llewellyn, 2000.

Rain, Gwinevere. *Spellcraft for Teens: A Magickal Guide to Writing and Casting Spells.* St. Paul, MN: Llewellyn, 2002.

Ravenwolf, Silver. *Solitary Witch: The Ultimate Book of Shadows for the New Generation.* St. Paul, MN: Llewellyn, 2003.

Ravenwolf, Silver. *Teen Witch Kit: Everything You Need to Make Magick.* St. Paul, MN: Llewellyn, 2000.

Sabrina, Lady. *Wiccan Magick for Beginners: A Guide to Spells, Rites, and Customs.* New York: Kensington Publishing Corp., 2001.

Wood, Jamie. *The Teen Spellbook: Magick for Young Witches.* Berkeley, CA: Celestial Arts, 2001.

Zimmermann, Denise and Katherine Gleason. *The Complete Idiot's Guide to Wicca and Witchcraft.* New York: Alpha Books, 2000.

About the Author

Gwinevere Rain has been a Wiccan practitioner since the age of fourteen. Her first book, *Spellcraft for Teens*, sparked her writing career and initiated a desire to show others the beauty of ethical magick.

Motivated by her own spirituality and belief in intuition, Gwinevere wrote her second book, *Moonbeams & Shooting Stars,* which is a multifaith guide for teen women. She has been featured in *Seventeen* magazine (November 2002) and runs her own website:

www.Gothic-Rain.com.

In her spare time she loves to curl up with a good book, write in her journal, or create jewelry.

About the Photography

The photography presented within this guide was a harmonious effort between Gwinevere and her mother, Ann. The images were achieved with Kodak 400-speed black-and-white film and a professional Pentax camera.

Gwinevere oversaw each photo session and incorporated her personal findings, belongings, and treasures within each shot. This unique endeavor between Gwinevere and her mother contributes to the positive energy and inspiration within this book.

Ann has a bachelor of science degree in graphics and fine art, and achieved her master's degree from Stony Brook University, Long Island.